Bayard Taylor

Japan in our Days

Bayard Taylor

Japan in our Days

ISBN/EAN: 9783742835581

Manufactured in Europe, USA, Canada, Australia, Japa

Cover: Foto ©Andreas Hilbeck / pixelio.de

Manufactured and distributed by brebook publishing software (www.brebook.com)

Bayard Taylor

Japan in our Days

ILLUSTRATED LIBRARY OF TRAVEL

JAPAN

IN OUR DAY

COMPILED AND ARRANGED BY

BAYARD TAYLOR

NEW YORK
CHARLES SCRIBNER'S SONS
743 & 745 BROADWAY
1881

COPYRIGHT BY
CHARLES SCRIBNER'S SONS
1891

PREFATORY NOTE.

THE rapid change in the policy of the Japanese government, which is now opening the Empire to the arts and ideas of modern civilization, has been followed by a corresponding increase in our knowledge of the Japanese institutions and people. The compiler's object has been to select all that is newest and most interesting in the works of recent visitors to Japan, in order to make this volume a tolerably complete gallery of pictures, representing the life and customs of the Japanese at this time. Many strange and peculiar features of that life will very soon pass away, and already some of the experiences related by Sir Rutherford Alcock and M. Humbert could not be repeated. It is believed, therefore, that the information contained in this volume will be found not only attractive in itself, but convenient as a standard by which to measure the great changes which science and the mechanic arts will effect in the condition of the Japanese Empire.

CONTENTS.

CHAPTER I.
EARLIEST INTERCOURSE WITH JAPAN . . . 1

CHAPTER II.
JAPANESE HISTORY 8

CHAPTER III.
THE OPENING OF JAPAN 20

CHAPTER IV.
ALCOCK'S ASCENT OF FUSI-YAMA 28

CHAPTER V.
ALCOCK'S OVERLAND JOURNEY FROM NAGASAKI TO YEDO   40

CHAPTER VI.
M. HUMBERT'S VOYAGE FROM NAGASAKI TO YEDO . 56

CHAPTER VII.
RESIDENCE AT YOKOHAMA . . 63

CHAPTER VIII.
EXCURSION TO KAMAKURA 74

CHAPTER IX.
THE HIGHWAY TO YEDO 89

CHAPTER X.
LIFE IN YEDO 95

CHAPTER XI.
WALKS IN YEDO 105

CHAPTER XII.
THE RESIDENCE OF THE TYCOONS . . 123

CHAPTER XIII.
THE COURT AND ITS REVENUES . . 134

CHAPTER XIV.
THE CITIZENS' QUARTER . . . 138

CHAPTER XV.
THE BRIDGES OF YEDO. — THE POLICE . 150

CHAPTER XVI.
THE HONDJO 158

CHAPTER XVII.
JAPANESE ART AND INDUSTRY . . . 164

CHAPTER XVIII.
THE LITERATURE OF THE JAPANESE . . 170

CHAPTER XIX.
RECREATIONS AND DOMESTIC CUSTOMS OF THE JAPANESE . 180

CHAPTER XX.
SOJOURN IN THE HARBOR 192

CHAPTER XXI.
JAPANESE FESTIVALS AND THEATRES . . . 199

CHAPTER XXII
VARIETIES OF JAPANESE LIFE . . . 209

CHAPTER XXIII.
THE GYMNASTS AND WRESTLERS . . 215

CHAPTER XXIV.
Scenes around Yedo 224

CHAPTER XXV.
New-year's Day in Yedo 237

CHAPTER XXVI.
The Japanese and their Mythology 249

CHAPTER XXVII.
The Literary Age of Japan 258

CHAPTER XXVIII.
Popular Superstitions 266

CHAPTER XXIX
The New Order of Things in Japan 273

LIST OF ILLUSTRATIONS.

	PAGE
Fire Fishing in the Bay of Yedo	Frontispiece.
Fusi-yama	28
Entrance to a Japanese Tavern	30
Climbing the Cone of Fusi-yama	36
Simonoséki	45
Entrance to the Harbor of Hiogo	46
Daimios	50
Japanese Bettos	64
Japanese Ladies going to pay a Visit	66
Japanese crossing a Mountain Gorge	71
Japanese Tea House	77
Japanese Pilgrims	83
A Street Scene in Japan	91
Entrance to the American Legation, Yedo	95
American Legation, Yedo	99
Noon Scene on a Japanese Canal	105
Little Jugglers in the Streets of Yedo	108
Japanese Blacksmiths	110
Soldier of the Tycoon	118
A Parricide on the Way to Execution	133
A Japanese Stable	138
Japanese Cook	144
Japanese Restaurant at Yedo	146
Priest of the Higher Grade	160
A Japanese School	170
Countryman. Winter Costume	180
Citizen of Yedo. Winter Costume	183

LIST OF ILLUSTRATIONS

	PAGE
JAPANESE MARRIAGE	184
THE MIKADO OF JAPAN	192
FETE OF THE SEA-GOD	197
NEW YEAR'S FESTIVITIES	199
JAPANESE FESTIVAL OF THE BANNERS	200
PROCESSION OF THE WHITE ELEPHANT	201
JAPANESE THEATRE — SCENES BEFORE THE CURTAIN	202
JAPANESE THEATRE — SCENES BEHIND THE CURTAIN	206
TORTOISE CHARMER	208
JAPANESE WRESTLERS	215
JAPANESE FEATS AT BALANCING	248

TRAVELS IN JAPAN.

CHAPTER I.

EARLIEST INTERCOURSE WITH JAPAN.

ALTHOUGH the history of the Japanese, as an organized and civilized people, extends back beyond the Christian era, the ancient geographers were ignorant of the very existence of the Empire. The first notice of Japan ever given to the world is found in the travels of Marco Polo, who heard of the country, under the name of Zipangu, at the court of Kublaï Khan (in Peking), at the close of the thirteenth century. This is his brief description: —

"Zipangu is an island in the Eastern Ocean, situate at the distance of about 1,500 miles from the mainland of *Manji* [Mantchooria?]. It is of considerable size; its inhabitants have fair complexions, are well made, and are civilized in their manners. Their religion is the worship of idols. They are independent of every foreign power, and governed only by their kings. They have gold in the greatest abundance, its sources being inexhaustible; but as the king does not allow of its being exported, few merchants visit the country, nor is it frequented by much shipping from other ports. To this circumstance we are to attribute the extraordinary richness of the sovereign's palace, according to what we are told by those who have had access to the place. The entire roof is covered with a plating of gold, in the same manner as we cover houses, or more properly churches, with lead. The ceilings of the halls are of the same precious metal; many of the apartments have small tables of pure gold, considerably thick, and the windows also have golden ornaments. So vast, indeed, are the riches of the palace, that it is impossible to convey an idea of them. In this island there are pearls also in large quantities, of a red color, round in shape and of great size; equal in value to, or even exceeding, that of the white pearls. It is customary with one part of the inhabitants to bury their dead, and with another part to burn them. The former have a practice of putting one of these pearls into the mouth of the corpse. There are also found there a number of precious stones.

"Of so great celebrity was the wealth of this island, that a desire was excited in the breast of the Grand Khan Kublaï, now reigning, to make the conquest of it, and to annex it to his dominions."

Japan was first really discovered — that is, made known to Europe from actual observation — fifty years after the discovery of America. In the year 1542, a Portuguese vessel, bound for Macao, was driven far out of her course by a tempest, and finally arrived in the harbor of Bungo, on the Japanese island of Kiusiu, the most southerly of the five great islands of the Empire. Although the Japanese, on account of their previous wars with China, were cautious and vigilant in their intercourse with foreigners, there was no prohibition of such intercourse, and the Portuguese were kindly received. The latter took advantage of their accident, and made a treaty with the Prince of Bungo, by which a Portuguese vessel was to be sent every year, for the purposes of commerce. Seven years later, several Jesuit priests, among them the distinguished Francis Xavier, went to Japan, in order to undertake the conversion of the people. They were heartily welcomed, not only in the province of Bungo, but throughout the entire country. The Portuguese were as free to preach as to trade, and for twenty years, or more, both avocations flourished without interruption. In the year 1585, an embassy of seven Japanese Christians visited Rome, and by the end of the century the number of converts was estimated at two hundred thousand. The Portuguese trade, through the ports of Bungo, Firando, and Nagasaki, became so lucrative that Macao rose to be one of the wealthiest cities of the East.

In April, 1600, the first Dutch vessel, piloted by an English sailor named William Adams, reached Japan. After some delay and suspicion on the part of the Japanese, the Dutch captain was allowed to dispose of his cargo and leave, but Adams was retained, on account of his knowledge of mathematics and shipbuilding. He was very well treated, but remained a compulsory resident of Japan, until his death, twenty years later. Meanwhile the Dutch had followed up their advantage, and maintained a limited trade through the port of Firando, in spite of the protestations of the Portuguese. The English, also, while Adams was yet living, obtained the same privilege, but their commercial intercourse was slight, and was finally discontinued, because it did not prove very profitable.

The persecution of the native Christians by the Japanese Government had already commenced. It appears that the Franciscan and Dominican orders had followed in the wake of the Jesuits, and that the jealousy of these three sects, together with their increasing defiance of the Japanese authority, had given rise to frequent and serious troubles. Crosses, shrines, and churches were erected in prohibited places; religious processions were led through the very streets of Miako, and the hostility of the government needlessly provoked in other ways. Once thoroughly aroused, it manifested itself in the most inhuman forms. Nevertheless after the massacres of 1612 and 1614, the Portuguese continued to import missionaries, in violation of the Imperial order; whereupon their intercourse with Japan was restricted to the little island of Desima, in the harbor of Nagasaki.

The closing episode of this history was brought about by the capture of a Portuguese vessel off the Cape of Good Hope, by the Dutch. Among other things found on board the prize, there were certain treasonable letters to the King of Portugal, written by a native Japanese, who had long been a principal agent of the Portuguese in the country, and was a devout Catholic. These letters (according to Dutch authority) revealed a plot by which the Portuguese were to unite with the Japanese Christians, overturn the old empire and establish a new and Christian dynasty. The Dutch Government immediately dispatched these documents to Japan: it was a welcome opportunity of overthrowing the influence of their hated rivals, and securing for themselves the monopoly of trade. The evidence on both sides must be received with caution; indeed, in this whole history, we can only be certain in regard to the results. The Japanese agent denied the authorship of the letters, which the Portuguese also assert to have been Dutch forgeries; but the former was burned at the stake, and an imperial proclamation was issued (in 1637) decreeing that "the whole race of the Portuguese, with their mothers, nurses, and whatever belongs to them, shall be banished forever."

The same proclamation set forth that no Japanese ship or boat, or any native of Japan, should henceforth presume to quit the country under pain of forfeiture and death; that any Japanese returning from a foreign country should be put to death; that no nobleman or soldier should be suffered to purchase anything of a foreigner; that any person presuming to bring a letter from abroad, or to return to Japan after he had been banished, should die, with all his family, and that whoever presumed to intercede for such offenders should be put to death; that all persons who propagated the doctrines of the Christians or bore that scandalous name, should be seized and imprisoned as felons, — with many other provisions of the same nature. This was the beginning of the exclusive system of Japan, which was maintained for a little more than two hundred years.

The final persecution and extermination of the Japanese Christians followed this decree. The town of Simabara, in which they had taken refuge, was battered down by the aid of Dutch cannon, and a general slaughter followed. This was the end of Catholic Christianity in Japan. But the Dutch, instead of obtaining more liberal conditions of trade in return for their services, were obliged to be content with the same limitation of intercourse which had previously been imposed upon the Portuguese. They were restricted to the little island of Desima, six hundred feet in length by two hundred and forty in breadth, in the harbor of Nagasaki, and thus, just a hundred years after the first discovery of Japan, the isolation of the Empire was established. Kämpfer, writing at the close of the seventeenth century, says, " In short, by our humble complaisance and connivance, we were so far from bringing this proud and jealous nation to any greater confidence, or more intimate friendship, that, on the contrary, their jealousy and mistrust seemed to increase from that time. They both hated and despised us for what we had done. In the year 1641, soon after the total expulsion of the Portuguese and the suppression of Christianity among the natives, we were ordered to quit our comfortable factory at Firando, and to confine ourselves, under a very rigid inspection, to the small islet of Desima, which is more like a prison than a factory. So great was the covetousness of the Dutch, and so strong the alluring power of Japanese gold, that, rather than quit the prospect of a trade (indeed most advantageous) they willingly underwent an almost perpetual imprisonment, for such, in fact, is our residence at Desima, and chose to suffer many hardships in a foreign and heathen country, to be remiss in performing divine service on Sundays and solemn festivals, to leave off praying and singing of psalms and all the outer signs of Christianity ; and lastly, patiently and submissively to bear the abusive and injurious behavior of these proud infidels toward us."

Having once accepted the conditions, however, the Dutch continued to observe them. The residence on Desima was burdened with restrictions, some of which were positively degrading: the trade was limited to two vessels a year, and the privilege of an annual journey to Yedo was afterwards changed to a journey once in four years. The best reason which can be given for the continuation, by the Japanese government, of a privilege of such slight commercial importance, must be found in that curiosity which is such an important element in the character of the race. Although determined to isolate themselves from the rest of the world, they were still anxious to know what was going on in other nations; and when the empire was finally opened to general intercourse, there was already a class of officials sufficiently well informed to comprehend the extent and importance of the new relations which the government had assumed.

CHAPTER II.

JAPANESE HISTORY.

KÄMPFER, Klaproth, and other earlier writers have given outlines of the history of Japan, from such materials as were accessible to them. Like that of China, and other ancient Asiatic nations, the thread of actual events is so blended with fable and fiction that it is no easy matter to separate it: the further we recede in the past the more confused becomes the narrative, until we finally reach a point where everything is uncertain. The most recent of the works on this subject has been compiled with the aid of an intelligent Japanese scholar,[1] and offers a much clearer and more probable narrative than we find in any of its predecessors.

The traditional or fabulous portion of Japanese history extends beyond our era; but it will only be necessary to note those prominent characters or events, which may be accepted as having a basis of fact. The first of the noted historical personages is Yamato, who is supposed to have lived during the second century. He was a famous military chieftain, belonging to the imperial family, and achieved the conquest of the eastern and northern portions of the island of

[1] *Japan; Being a Sketch of the History, Government, and Officers of the Empire.* By Walter Dickson. William Blackwood and Sons, Edinburgh, 1869.

Nipon. He left a son, whose widow, the Empress Jingu, is another famous historical character. She conquered Corea and made it tributary to Japan, in the third century, suppressed a powerful rebellion in Kiusiu, and left a well established empire to her son O-sin. During the reign of the latter, Chinese letters are said to have been introduced into Japan, and about the same period the Buddhist faith began to displace the older Sinto religion, which consisted chiefly of prayers, without any distinct idea of a Being to whom to pray, except that white paper, or a mirror, was used as a symbol of purity. The Buddhist faith not only included this, but supplied, in addition, the idea of a pure life, and final absorption into the Deity, through self-denial. Hence it spread very rapidly; and its introduction, by way of China, brought with it various Chinese customs, which somewhat modified the Japanese institutions, such as the degrees of rank among government officials.

There were other wars with Corea about the middle of the seventh century, and about the same time the northern island of Yeso was brought under subjection to Japan. The capital of the empire, which was then divided into eight provinces, some of which were usually in a state of revolt, was fixed at Miako, about the year 800. For three or four centuries after this, the history of Japan is that of several of its prominent families, the members of which successively acquired the imperial power. The principal of them are the Fusiwara, Sungawara, Minnamoto, and Tatchibanna. Their rivalry, of course, gave rise to violent civil wars, during which certain individuals acquired power and fame, but the condition of the country and people did not greatly improve. There were no serious difficulties, either with Corea or China, after this time; but the central power seems to have been based upon no firm and permanent system, and thus was in constant danger of being overthrown.

During the twelfth century there was a memorable struggle between the Minnamoto and the Hé or Taira family. In the first great battle the latter obtained the victory, and Kio Mori, its chief, received the government of a province. He became prime minister, and one of the most energetic and unscrupulous which Japan had ever known. After the death of the emperor, the latter's successor, a mere boy, married the daughter of Kio Mori, who was practically the ruler for ten years. He died in 1181, leaving a noble name in Japanese history. After his death, however, the rival family, the Minnamoto, overthrew the Hé dynasty, and exterminated, as was then supposed, every one who bore the name. In the centre of the island of Kiusiu, there is a high table-land, partly marsh, from twenty to thirty miles in diameter. According to Japanese accounts, the interior of this district was utterly unknown, a hundred years ago, when the discovery was accidentally made that there were people living in three villages in the midst of this marsh. Further investigations having been made, it was found that these people were the remnants of the Hé family, who had fled thither six hundred years before, and had there isolated themselves, through fear of destruction! They had taught their own fears to their children, and the remote descendants, when found, were overwhelmed with the dread of some terrible punishment.

The Minnamoto emperor, Yoritomo, lived at Kamakura (not far from the present foreign settlement at Kanagawa), where the ruins of his palace are still to be seen. He died in 1199, and is generally regarded by the Japanese as the greatest hero in their history. Kamakura was the capital for a long time, and even in the time of the Jesuits, when Yedo had succeeded to the distinction. the population still numbered 20,000. In the time of Kublaï Khan (about 1281), Japan was summoned to pay tribute to China, and a large military force was sent to enforce the demand. The Japanese chronicles relate that this "invincible armada" was scattered by a storm, 30,000 men drowned or slain after reaching the shore, and the ambassadors of Kublaï Khan beheaded.

The fourteenth and fifteenth centuries are chronicles of civil war, with occasional changes in the relation of the imperial authority to the independent princes; but all is shifting, unstable, weak, and we find no evidence that the natural resources of the islands were greatly developed during this period. But the last period of transition in Japanese history (except that in our own day) was at hand, and destined to be coeval with the earliest intercourse with Europeans. The same year (1542) which witnessed the arrival of the first Portuguese vessel, gave birth to Iyeyas. in some respects the greatest man Japan ever produced. The native historians give the year 1552 as that when Christianity was first introduced at Bungo by foreigners from the south. This is evidently an error, as St. Francis Xavier died in 1551, after two years spent as a missionary in Japan.

"The period at which this event [the introduction of Christianity] took place," says Mr. Dickson, "is worthy of note. Japan had been for years torn by rival factions, and by the contests of men intriguing for power. The emperor was powerless, and reduced by poverty and neglect to a position bordering on contempt. The eastern court at Kamakura retained some portions of its former power, and was at least a hot-bed where schemes might be hatched for overthrowing either the power of the court of Miako, or that of some of the neighboring princes. Yedo was almost unknown, except as a village dependency of the castle. The western provinces were under the sway of independent chiefs, while the island of Kiusiu hardly acknowledged the sway of the Mikado. A small beginning of commerce with China had been going on for several years past, and was transacted at Ningpo. It was not likely, therefore, that at the first landing upon Tanegasima the country and people of Japan were unknown to the Portuguese buccaneers upon the coast of China. If Mendez Pinto is to be credited, there were eight hundred Portuguese then living near Ningpo under their own laws; but if his account of the doings of his countrymen in China be correct — and it is in many respects corroborated by concurrent testimony, — the men who sailed about those seas were not exactly the men best suited to spread a healthy commerce, or to propagate correct notions of the Christian religion."

The freedom allowed to the first Jesuit missionaries is partly explained by the distracted condition of the empire at that time. The central power was too weak to assert any particular authority, and the rival factions too seriously engaged to notice an innovation, in which they probably saw no danger. It was not until about 1570 that the chief, Nobu Nanga, succeeded in establishing his power, and thus restoring some degree of order. He was joined by Iyeyas, still a young man, but already noted for his great administrative abilities. Nobu Nanga first commenced a crusade against the Buddhist priests, who were equally powerful and arrogant. He took from them the great castle of Osacca, which had been one of their principal temples, and for a time encouraged the Jesuits for his own purposes. He overthrew the power of many families, and made his will supreme throughout the empire, although he was never the actual ruler.

By the year 1582, Nobu Nanga had subjugated nearly the whole of Japan. He built a splendid temple, placed his own statue therein, and caused divine honors to be paid to it. Returning to Miako immediately afterwards, he was suddenly surrounded while attended only by a small guard, and assassinated by the soldiers of a noble whom he had insulted. He was forty-nine years of age at his death. Taikosama, who succeeded to the imperial power, and Iyeyas, already governor of eight provinces, were his two generals. The former was a man of low birth and misshapen form, who had risen by his native daring of character and great military talent. Iyeyas, who was his superior in talent, and possibly in influence, was one of those men who never undertake to hasten what they feel to be their ultimate destiny. He only resisted Taikosama's pretensions sufficiently to make himself properly respected, and then acquiesced in the cunning emperor's rule.

The reign of Taikosama, which lasted until 1598, is notable chiefly for an invasion of Corea, at first successful, but with no final result, and for his course toward the Christians, both native and foreign. He at first encouraged the latter, following the policy of his predecessor; but when the Buddhist temples were burned, the priests assailed, and the new sect showed itself as haughty and intolerant as the old, he began to adopt measures of repression. The five Franciscan monks, whom he ordered to be executed at Nagasaki in 1587, had repeatedly violated his commands and defied his authority; the Jesuit writers, themselves, attribute to the Franciscans the responsibility of the persecution of the Japanese Christians.

The same policy seems to have influenced Iyeyas, who succeeded Taikosama, and reigned until 1616. He was a leader of remarkable military genius, who never hesitated to engage a force double his own, and very rarely knew what it was to be defeated. Every revolt against his authority was suppressed, and he remained, for eighteen years, supreme ruler of Japan. The fact that the Christians took sides against him in the great rebellion of 1600, goes far to account for his later severity toward them. Nevertheless, even the Jesuit writers give Iyeyas credit for the moderation and sagacity with which he exercised his power. He pardoned as frequently as he punished; his great aim seems to have been to establish a central authority strong enough to control the semi-independent provinces, and thereby both strengthen the power and favor the development of the Japanese race.

Iyeyas may be considered as the founder of Yedo. The earlier capital of Kamakura had fallen into decay. A part of the present castle of Yedo was already in existence, and, curiously enough, on a summer-house in the garden attached to it there was engraved a stanza, which is now looked upon by the Japanese as a prophecy of coming events, finally accomplished in our day: —

> "From this window I look upon Fusi-yama,
> With its snow of a thousand years:
> To my gate ships will come from the far East,
> Ten thousand miles."

Mr. Dickson says: "Considering the associations which hung around Miako and Narra and Osacca as the capitals, imperial, ecclesiastical, and commercial, of the empire, it might be deemed a great stretch of power and firm confidence in himself and the stability of his system of government, that Iyeyas should think of removing the seat of the executive to Yedo. He had doubtless pondered long and deeply over the best system of government for the country. He had seen the anarchy which preceded the rise of Nobu Nanga to power; he had seen the want of system by which the structure of government at that time had crumbled down with the fall of the one man upon whose shoulders it had been supported; he had all the experience since that time to be gained from ruling an extensive territory of his own, combined with what observations he might make upon the system of Taikosama. In the settling of that system, doubtless, he had a large share; but he went further than Taikosama, and, disregarding the old associations connected with Miako, he removed the seat of the executive to his own provinces and to his own court in the city of Yedo, in what was considered a remote part of the empire, the inhabitants of which were looked upon as rude and unpolished. The city, when Iyeyas first took possession of the castle, consisted only of one street. It increased very much in size under his care, and through the residence of the court, the daimios, and their wives and families; and in no long time became a city of great commercial importance."

The Jesuit writers, in 1607, state that 300,000 workmen were then employed upon the imperial castle in Yedo.

When Iyeyas died, he left his son Hidetada as his successor; but his most valuable legacy to Japan was his code of laws, or rather rules of political action, which were added to the older laws already in practice, but did not wholly supersede them. This code, which is partly drawn from the works of Confucius and Mencius, is characterized by great shrewdness and knowledge of human nature. Many of the one hundred rules apply to existing institutions or habits of society, and have therefore only a local importance; but there are some of a general nature, which might be profitably adopted by all nations. Take, for instance, the following: —

1. "When I was young I determined to fight and punish all my own and my ancestors' enemies, and I did punish them; but afterwards, by deep consideration, I found that the way of heaven was to help the people, and not to punish them. Let my successors

follow out this policy, or they are not of my line. In this lies the strength of the nation."

2. "There are men who always say Yes, and there are others who sometimes say No. Now, the former I wish to put away from me, and the latter I wish to be near me. The elders of the Gorogin are to examine and see that men do not do such business only as is agreeable to them, and avoid all that is the reverse. I wish to have about me all opinions of men, both those who differ from me and those who agree with me."

3. "The master of men must know what each is useful for. Men are like instruments: one cannot do the work of a chisel with a hammer; one cannot make a small hole with a saw, but a gimlet must be used. The principle is the same as to men. Men with brains are to be used for work requiring brains; men of strong frame for work requiring strength; men of strong heart for work requiring courage. *Weak men are to be put in poor places.* Every man in his proper place. There are places for weak men and places for fools. Soldiers are to be chosen on these principles, so that with a thousand men in one body, the whole may act together and the empire have peace. This is always to be kept in memory."

Iyeyas further records that he has fought ninety battles, and has had eighteen narrow escapes from death, — wherefore he erected eighteen splendid temples, in different parts of the empire. From his rules concerning intercourse with foreigners, we quote the following passages: —

1. "If any representative of a foreign nation comes

to the country, the officers must take care that everything is in good order; that horses and horse-furniture be good, the houses and roads clean. If they are dirty, it can be seen at a glance whether the nation is prosperous or the reverse."

2. "If a foreign vessel should be wrecked on the shore of Japan, the officers of government are to be immediately informed, and an interpreter is to be sent to ask what they require. Sometimes the officer may be required to be strict and severe, at other times hospitable and kind. The vessel is to be watched and no trading allowed."

These laws of Iyeyas, and the additional measures which he enforced during the eighteen years of his reign, really accomplished the great ends he had in view, — that of establishing his own family in power, and preserving the internal peace of the empire. In the year 1806 a grand national festival was held in Japan, when the nobles and people congratulated the emperor on the remarkable fact — to which there is no parallel in the history of any other nation, — that the empire had enjoyed an unbroken peace for nearly two hundred years. During this time the internal resources of the country had been highly developed; Yedo had grown to be one of the great cities of the world; the isolation of Japan had been scrupulously respected by more civilized nations; and the restrictions imposed upon the people had grown, by inheritance, to be a natural accompaniment of their lives.

Except a rebellion of no extent or importance, in 1838, the Japanese annals record nothing of much more interest than fires, earthquakes, or showers of meteoric stones, until the commencement of intercourse with foreign nations, in our day. From this time, the history of Japan will be associated with that of the United States, England, and Russia, in the development of civilization.

CHAPTER III.

THE OPENING OF JAPAN.

AFTER the expulsion of the Portuguese and the confinement of the Dutch to the little island of Desima, in the harbor of Nagasaki, no serious attempt was made, for two hundred years, by any great commercial nation, to enter into relations with Japan. The English, in 1673, applied for permission to trade, but the captain of the vessel was immediately asked by the Japanese officials, whether his king had not married the daughter of the King of Portugal? This information had been furnished to them by the Dutch, who seem to have constantly made use of their exclusive opportunities to prejudice the Japanese against other European nations.

A small embassy, sent from Okhotsk in 1793, by order of the Empress Catherine II. was repelled, though in a courteous manner. Several English vessels made separate attempts to trade, about the same time, with similar results, the Japanese exhibiting the greatest decision and firmness in their policy, yet being careful to avoid giving cause for retaliation. Even in their imprisonment of the Russian Captain Golownin and his men, in 1812 and 1813, they seem to have avoided all wanton harshness. Their conduct, in short, gave rise to a general belief in the great strength of their nation and its defenses, and undoubtedly contributed to postpone the enforcement of a nearer intercourse, until the progress of steam navigation and the use of heavier artillery furnished other countries with the means of supporting their representatives by adequate physical power.

A rather singular attempt was made by the English, in 1808. During the summer of that year, a ship under Dutch colors entered the harbor of Nagasaki. The Dutch Governor of Desima, M. Doeff, who was expecting the usual trader, sent one of his subordinates on board. As the latter did not return, the suspicions of M. Doeff and the Japanese Governor of Nagasaki were excited, and for a day or two various plans were discussed, of burning the strange vessel by means of a fire-ship, of closing the mouth of the harbor by sinking junks filled with stones, etc. But, before any plan could be carried into execution, the ship, which was the English frigate *Phæton*, hoisted anchor and sailed away, leaving the Japanese governor and his principal officers under the necessity of committing suicide.

In the summer of 1813, two vessels, apparently Dutch, arrived at Nagasaki. They were, in fact, dispatched from Batavia by Sir Stamford Raffles, the English Governor of Java, who sent with them M. Waardenaar, a former Governor of Desima, to replace M. Doeff, who, having been cut off from the world for four years, was entirely ignorant that Java had temporarily passed out of the hands of Holland. Nevertheless, on learning the facts, he refused to comply with the order, or to acknowledge the authority by which his successor was appointed. It was impossible to compel him; for the Japanese authorities would have answered his application by destroying the two English vessels. An arrangement was made by which the trade was conducted in the usual manner, the ships being allowed to depart, and M. Doeff retaining possession of Desima, for Holland. The cunning scheme of Sir Stamford Raffles was thus baffled.

Captain Gordon, in 1818, and Sir Edward Belcher, in 1845, visited ports in Japan, but were warned off and not allowed any intercourse with the shore. Before the latter date, however, the first American attempt had been made to establish intercourse. In 1831, a Japanese junk was blown out to sea, and after drifting about for a long time, at length went ashore near the mouth of the Columbia River. Kindness was shown to the shipwrecked Japanese, and finally they were carried to Macao, where they received the protection and care of the American and English residents. It was decided to return them to their home, as a means of attempting communication. Accordingly the ship *Morrison* was fitted out by the American house of King & Co. for the voyage to Japan, all her armament being removed, to demonstrate her pacific mission. But, on reaching the bay of Yedo, the Japanese no sooner ascertained that the vessel was unarmed than they opened fire upon her. She then made a second attempt, in the harbor of Kagosima (in the island of Kiusiu), but was driven off by a battery on shore, and forced to return to China with the Japanese exiles.

The first expedition was sent by the United States to Japan in 1846. It consisted of the ship-of-the-line *Columbus,* and the corvette *Vincennes,* under command of Commodore Biddle. The expedition remained ten days in the bay of Yedo, the ships constantly surrounded by four hundred Japanese guardboats, filled with soldiers. No one was allowed to land, and the Emperor's answer to the President's letter consisted of the single sentence: "No trade can be allowed with any country except Holland."

The visit of the frigate *Preble,* in 1849, was of a different character. Information had reached the Government of the United States that sixteen American seamen, who had been shipwrecked on the Japanese coast, were kept as prisoners in the country, and Captain Glynn of the China squadron was sent to Nagasaki with the *Preble* to demand their release. On entering the harbor, a number of large boats attempted to prevent the frigate's further advance ; but she sailed boldly through them to a good anchorage. The hills around soon swarmed with soldiers, and sixty cannon, in batteries, were trained to bear on the *Preble's* decks. The tone of the Japanese authorities was haughty and defiant, but Captain Glynn met them with a determined spirit, demanding the immediate release of the prisoners. At the end of two days the latter were sent on board, and the frigate returned to China.

Early in 1852, the Government of the United States determined to make a formal application to that of Japan to establish intercourse between the two nations, and to dispatch it by a fleet sufficiently large and well-appointed to insure a proper reception. Twelve vessels, including supply ships, were designated for the service, and Commodore M. C. Perry was appointed to the command, with the necessary diplomatic powers. His flag-ship, the *Mississippi*, sailed from Norfolk in November, 1852, and the squadron was organized on the coast of China in the spring of 1853. After a visit to the Loo-Choo and Bonin Islands, Commodore Perry reached the bay of Yedo in July, and had an interview with two commissioners, appointed by the Emperor, at the town of Gori-hama, on the 14th of that month.

It is not necessary to enter into a minute relation of all the proceedings on this and the following occasion, when the first treaty was made. Commodore Perry adopted, at the outset, the only policy which could have been successful, combining firmness and courtesy with an assertion of dignity which the Japanese understood through their own customs. No interference with the vessels was permitted; the preliminary discussions were all conducted by naval officers of lower rank, the Commodore only making his appearance at the interview with the two princes; and the declarations of the power and importance of the American nation were skillfully coupled with expressions of friendship and respect for the Japanese. The point gained by this first visit was a courteous reception of the President's letter, and the establishment of pleasant personal relations with some of the chief Japanese officials.

The government having demanded time, for preparing an answer to the application, the fleet, after having visited the upper part of the bay, returned to China. The second visit was made in February, 1854, with the entire squadron. After rather tedious negotiations, it was agreed that the further conferences should be neld at Yokohama, and Commodore Perry landed tnere, the second time in Japan, on the 8th of March. The discussion with the commissioner appointed by the Emperor continued until the 23d, when a treaty was finally agreed upon, which was signed on the 31st. This treaty opened the ports of Simoda, in Nipon, and Hakodadi, in Yeso, to American vessels, permitting all necessary commerce, and the freedom of the country for a distance of seven Japanese miles from those ports. It was also stipulated that the United States should appoint consuls to reside in both places.

The success of the United States was immediately shared by England and Russia, whose expeditions reached Japan within a year after the acceptance of the American treaty. The conditions granted were similar, and the same advantages were, of course, extended by the Japanese Government to the Dutch. Thus the isolation of the empire from intercourse with the civilized world, which had lasted two hundred and fourteen years, was finally given up, and the long quiet of Japan was broken.

Mr. Townsend Harris, who was first appointed Consul to Simoda, succeeded, in 1858, in negotiating a commercial treaty, based upon that already made between the United States and China. This was a great advance upon the concessions obtained by Commodore Perry, through the exercise of the greatest patience and prudence. Fortunately, no troubles had arisen in the mean time; the ancient Japanese prejudice, finding that the first limited intercourse granted to foreigners was not followed by any unfavorable effects, yielded still further; and, as in the first instance, England, Holland, Russia, and France followed the course of the American representative. By this new treaty, Kanagawa, near Yedo, was made a port for commercial intercourse, and the ministers of foreign nations were permitted to reside in the capital. Mr. Harris, who had meanwhile been appointed Minister Resident, removed to Yedo, and remained there during the subsequent political conspiracies which had for their object the murder of the foreign residents, or their expulsion from Japan.

The first three or four years after the treaty of 1858 were a period of considerable danger. The Tycoon had been murdered, and the more conservative of the daimios, or native princes, were determined on a return to the old, exclusive policy of the empire. Mr. Harris's secretary was murdered in the streets of Yedo, the British Legation was attacked, the foreign residents at Kanagawa were in constant danger, and nothing but the firmness with which redress was demanded prevented the work already accomplished from being undone. When the Japanese Government finally agreed to send an embassy to the other powers, the change was virtually accepted. The policy of the predominant party is to preserve the friendship of other governments, and employ the science and skill of modern times in developing the resources of Japan. Hundreds of intelligent young Japanese, some of them belonging to the best families of the empire, have been sent to the United States to be educated; the commercial relations between the countries are constantly growing more extended and important, and former restrictions are gradually relaxing, as the people become familiar with the new order of things.

No oriental race shows such capacity for progress as the Japanese. One of their characteristics is a restless curiosity, which assists them in rapidly acquiring a knowledge of science and the mechanic arts ; and the eagerness which the government now exhibits to avail itself of all modern discoveries is all the more remarkable, since the opportunity was **so long and so stubbornly resisted.**

CHAPTER IV.

ALCOCK'S ASCENT OF FUSI-YAMA.

THE works of the old travellers, upon which, only twenty years ago, we were obliged to depend for our chief knowledge of Japan and the Japanese, are already obsolete. The writings of Kämpfer, Montanus, Thunberg, Titsingh, and more recently of Von Siebold, contain much that is valuable, and also much that is true at the present day; but the reader always prefers, if possible, to see a strange country through the eyes of his contemporaries. Since the opening of Japan many works have appeared, in addition to the multitudes of letters which have been sent from the country to the principal journals of America and Europe. By far the most careful and complete is that of M. Aimé Humbert, who was sent as Minister to Yedo by the Republic of Switzerland. Very interesting works, of a special scientific character, have been published by Fortune and Adams, and the two volumes of Sir Rutherford Alcock contain many particulars of the first years of intercourse which are not found elsewhere.

We propose to select some of the principal episodes of recent travel in the interior of Japan, before giving those illustrations of Japanese life, laws, and manners, which M. Humbert has collected. Sir Rutherford

FUSI-YAMA

Alcock's ascent of the great extinct volcano of Fusiyama, the sacred mountain of Japan, deserves the first notice. This isolated cone, towering high above all the mountains of the coast, is the prominent feature of the scenery on entering the bay of Yedo. Its snowy summit first catches the dawn, and it flames in the sky after the beautiful green shores of the bay are dusky in twilight. The journey to the summit is a religious pilgrimage for the men of Japan; the women according to a singular custom, only being allowed to ascend it every sixtieth year.

There are but two months — July and August — when the mountain is sufficiently free from snow to permit the ascent. The authorities at Yedo made so many attempts to prevent Sir Rutherford from carrying out his design, that he was not able to leave before the beginning of September, 1860. The journey was not absolutely prohibited, because the foreign ministers at Yedo claimed the right of travelling in the country; but every possible pretext was employed, first to discourage and then to delay the expedition, — probably in the hope that an early snow-fall might render the mountain inaccessible. After every plea had been exhausted, the Japanese accepted the inevitable with a good grace, but insisted on sending a large retinue of native officers and servants, including spies.

The party consisted of eight Europeans and nearly a hundred Japanese, with thirty horses. For the first fifty miles the road skirts the shore of the bay, crossing several peninsulas. As far as the town of Yosiwara, it is the *Tokaido*, or great high-road, connecting Yedo with the principal cities of Nipon. By this road all the southern daimios, or princes, annually travel to and from the court, generally with a retinue of several thousand retainers. They make, each day, from fifteen to twenty miles, halting at certain towns where there are large houses of entertainment built especially to accommodate them and the officers of the Tycoon. These houses are spacious, clean, and empty; the matted floor supplies at once a seat, a couch, and a table. Wadded counterpanes, and even mosquito nets, can generally be procured by the travellers.

"Immediately after arrival," says Sir Rutherford, "the landlord appears in full costume, and prostrating himself with his head to the ground, felicitates himself on the honor of receiving so distinguished a guest, begs to receive your orders, and that you will be pleased to accept a humble offering at his hands, — generally a little fruit, a few grapes or oranges, occasionally a rope of eggs, that is to say, a row of them, curiously twisted and plaited into a fine rope of straw. Due thanks having been given, he disappears, and you see no more of him or his servants — if, as usually happens, the guests bring their own and do not require help — until the foot is in the stirrup; when he makes another formal salutation, with parting thanks and good wishes. These details apply to the whole journey; the house or garden may be a little larger or smaller, the paper on the walls which divide the rooms a little fresher or dingier, but all the essential features are stereotyped, and exactly reproduced from one end of the kingdom to the other."

During the first few days the road lay over a succession of hills, of no great height, but from which

ENTRANCE TO A JAPANESE TAVERN.

fine views were obtained over the cultivated valleys on either side, with a background of mountains to the westward, among which Fusi-yama soared aloft in lonely grandeur. On the second day the river Saki had to be crossed. Here a body of strong porters is always in attendance, to carry travellers over on their shoulders. As they have a monopoly of the business, it must be lucrative ; but it has its drawbacks, for they are made responsible for the safety of travellers. If any accident happens to the latter, they have nothing left but to drown with them, for no excuses are taken. The English party paid about four dollars for the transfer, which occupied half an hour.

As this was the first foreign trip so far into the interior, it occasioned a great excitement in all the towns along the road. " As each roadside village, and even the larger towns, generally consist of one long and seemingly endless street, the news of our approach spread as rapidly and unerringly as the message of an electric telegraph, turning out the whole population as if by a simultaneous shock ; men, women, and children — clothed and nude, — dogs, poultry, and cats ! I think at Odowara no living thing could have been left inside. Such a waving sea of heads seemed to bar our passage, that I began to congratulate myself that my unknown friend, the Daimio, had so courteously provided me with an escort. I felt some curiosity as to the mode they would take to open a way through the dense mass of swaying bodies and excited heads, which looked all the more formidable the nearer we approached. My guides, however, seemed perfectly unembarrassed, and well they might be, — for when within a few steps of the foremost ranks, there was a wave of the fan and a single word of command issued, '*Shitanirio!*' (kneel down!) when, as if by magic, a wide path was opened and every head dropped; the body disappearing in some marvelous way behind the legs and knees of its owner."

After striking the foot of the Hakoni mountains, which rise to a height of six thousand feet above the sea, the road became a broad avenue of smooth gravel, winding through a succession of fertile plains and valleys, where the millet, buckwheat, and rice gave promise of rich harvests. The famous Hakoni Passes extend for a distance of twenty miles, and are so rough as to be nearly impassable. The travellers were obliged to dismount, while the grooms led the horses over slippery boulders, and up the channels torn by mountain torrents. The heights were covered with forests, principally of pine, inclosing fresh green valleys, beautifully cultivated, and watered by swift, clear streams. Here the *cryptomeria*, or Japanese cypress, grows to a height of one hundred and fifty feet, the hydrangea is a wild shrub, and the bamboo is found beside the oak and fir. Nothing can exceed the size, beauty, and variety of the vegetation.

After a long ascent, the party reached the little village of Yomotz, where there are hot saline springs, much frequented by the Japanese. A further journey of four hours through a furious rain brought the travellers to the lake and village of Hakoni. Here there is a government barrier, strictly guarded, both to prevent arms from being carried toward the capital, or any wife or female child of the daimios from traveling away from it, — the latter remaining as hostages while the princes visit their territories. The lake of Hakoni, which is a fine sheet of water, surrounded by hills — apparently the crater of an extinct volcano, — is 6,250 feet above the sea.

Beyond this lake there is a second barrier, at the highest point on the road, which then descends through a rich and populous country to the town of Missima, where the travellers passed the night. The next day brought them to Yosiwara, near the head of the deep gulf of Idzu, where they were obliged to leave the *Tokaido*, or high-road. A furious tempest detained them at Yosiwara for a day, during which time a messenger arrived from the Superior of the Buddhist monastery at Omio, high up on the side of Fusi-yama, offering the hospitality of his retreat. The next afternoon, they paid a short visit of ceremony, reserving a longer stay for the return, and pushed on before night to Mouriyama, the highest inhabited spot on the mountain.

By this time, all traces of the storm had vanished. The weather was pronounced favorable for the ascent by the Japanese, and the party started at daybreak, with three priests as guides and several strong mountain-men as porters. "At first," says Sir Rutherford, "our way lay through waving fields of corn, succeeded by a belt of high, rank grass; but soon we entered the mazes of the wood, which clings round the base and creeps high up the sides of the mountain, clothing the shoulders of the towering peak like the shaggy mane of a lion, with increased majesty. At first we found trees of large growth, — good trunks of the oak, the pine, and the beech, — and came upon many traces of the fury with which the typhoon had swept across. Large trees had been broken short off, and others uprooted. One of these broken off had been thrown right across our path, and compelled us either to scramble over or creep under its massive trunk. At Hakimondo we left the horses, and the last trace of permanent habitation or the haunts of men. Soon after the wood became thinner and more stunted in growth, while the beech and birch took the place of the oak and pine.

"We speedily lost all traces of life, vegetable or animal; a solitary sparrow or two alone flitted occasionally across our path. In the winding ascent over the rubble and scoriæ of the mountain — which alone is seen after ascending about half-way, — little huts or caves, as these resting-places are called, partly dug out and roofed over to give refuge to the pilgrims, appeared. There are, I think, eleven from Hakimondo to the summit, and they are generally about a couple of miles asunder. In one of these we took up our quarters for the night, and laid down our rugs, too tired to be very delicate. Nevertheless, the cold and the *occupants* we found former pilgrims had left, precluded much sleep. Daylight was rather a relief; and after a cup of hot coffee and a biscuit, we commenced the upper half of the ascent. The first part, after we left the horses, had occupied about four hours' steady work, and we reached our sleeping-station a little before sunset, lava and scoriæ everywhere around us. The clouds were sailing far below our feet, and a vast panorama of hill and plain, bounded by the sea, stretched far away. We looked down on the summits of the Hakoni range, being evidently far above their level, and we could distinctly see the lake lying in one of the hollows. The last half of the ascent is by far the most arduous, growing more steep as each station is passed.

" The first rays of the sun just touched, with a line of light, the broad waters of the Pacific as they wash the coast, when we made our start. The first station seemed very near, and was reached within the hour; but each step now became more difficult. The path, if such may be called the zigzag which our guides took, often led directly over fragments of out-jutting rocks, while the loose scoriæ prevented firm footing, and added much to the fatigue. The air became more rarefied, and perceptibly affected the breathing. At last the third station was passed, and a strong effort carried us to the fourth, the whole party by this time straggling at long intervals. This was now the last between us and the summit. It did not seem so far, until a few figures on the edge of the crater furnished a means of measurement, and they looked painfully diminutive.

" The last stage, more rough and precipitous than all the preceding, had this farther disadvantage, that it came after the fatigue of all the others. More than an hour's toil, with frequent stoppages for breath and rest to aching legs and spine, were needed; and more than one of our number felt very near the end of his strength before the last step placed the happy pilgrim on the topmost stone and enabled him to look down the yawning crater. This is a great oval opening, with jagged lips, estimated by Lieutenant Robinson, with such means of measurement as he could command, at about one thousand yards in length, with a mean width of six hundred, and is probably about three hundred and fifty yards in depth. Looking down on the other side, which had a northern aspect, there seemed a total absence of vegetation, even on the lower levels, and the rich country we had left was completely hid by a canopy of clouds drifting far below. The estimated height of the edge of the crater above the level of the sea was 13,997 feet; and the highest peak, 14,177 feet.

"The Japanese, who perform this pilgrimage from religious motives, are generally dressed in white garments, which they are careful to have stamped with various mystic characters and idols' images by the bonzes located there during the season for that purpose. On the sleeves of many of the pilgrims scallop-shells appear, — a strange coincidence, which I have never been able to explain. The origin of the pilgrimage is traced back to an ancient date, when a holy man, the founder of the Sinto religion — the oldest in Japan, — took up his residence on the mountain. Since his death, his spirit is still believed to have influence to bestow health and various other blessings on those who make the pilgrimage in honor of his memory.

"The volcano has long been extinct; the latest eruption recorded was in 1707. The tradition is that the mountain itself appeared in a single night from the bowels of the earth, a lake of equal dimensions making its appearance near Miako at the same hour. The time actually spent in climbing up to the summit was

CLIMBING THE CONE OF FUSI-YAMA.

about eight hours, but the descent occupied little more than three. We slept two nights on the mountain, and had greatly to congratulate ourselves on the weather, having fallen upon the only two fine days out of six. As we descended on the last morning there was a thick Scotch mist, which soon changed into a drenching rain. We only found patches of snow here and there near the summit, but on our return to Yedo, three weeks later, it was completely covered."

On their return, the travellers spent the night at the monastery of Omio, where they were treated with the greatest hospitality, the monks having even attempted to furnish seats in the European fashion, by nailing pieces of board over the tops of small tubs. The next day they retraced their road as far as the town of Missima, after fording a river so swollen by the rains as to be very dangerous. Here they turned aside from the main highway, in order to visit the mineral springs of Atami, on the shore of the promontory of Idzu. The country was very beautiful, diversified with clumps of trees, hedge-rows, and winding rivulets. Nothing could be richer than the soil, or the variety of its productions. Snug-looking hamlets and homesteads were nestled among the trees, or under the hills, and here and there were park walls, or splendid avenues of cryptomeria, leading to the residences of the native princes. The people had a happy, contented, and prosperous air, quite disproving the accounts of the oppression and exaction imposed upon them by their local rulers. The principal crop was rice, but there were also many fields of tobacco and cotton, arum and sweet potato, with orchards of persimmon and orange trees. In passing through these mountain districts, the travellers frequently came upon groups of peasantry, collected from all the surrounding hamlets for the purpose of seeing the strangers, — perhaps the greatest novelty of their lives. They sat upon some knoll, or small hillock by the roadside, or kneeling on their mats, patiently waiting the uncertain hour when the foreigners should appear.

In the afternoon Atami was reached, lying in a narrow gorge close to the shore, with the steam from its hot springs rising above the houses. The principal bathing establishment, reserved for the use of the daimios, had been prepared for the Minister's reception, and the accommodations, though simple, were found to be very comfortable. Atami has an agricultural and fishing population of only about 1,400. The people cultivate their fields of rice and millet, and a few vegetables; the bay provides them with mackerel, lobsters, and various kinds of fish peculiar to the coast. They use some of the hot springs for cooking, the water being saline, with a very slight trace of sulphur. The natives make use of the baths adjoining the spring, for rheumatism and for diseases of the skin and eyes.

Sir Rutherford Alcock and his party remained for three weeks in this isolated region. The villagers soon grew accustomed to their presence, and were as quiet and inoffensive as they could have desired. But they grew weary, at least, of the monotony of the life, and of the small chance afforded them in so remote a corner, of learning any important facts concerning the condition of the people. The only branch of manufacture at Atami is that of paper, which is made of the bark of three kinds of trees, and is of so firm a texture that it is almost impossible to tear it. The Japanese use it in place of linen, for handkerchiefs and other domestic purposes, and, when oiled, for waterproof capes and cloaks.

The return journey from Atami to Kanagawa, near Yedo, was made in three days, without any adventure worth noting. The trip, however, is of special interest as the first undertaken by a foreigner since the opening of Japan to intercourse with the world.

CHAPTER V.

ALCOCK'S OVERLAND JOURNEY FROM NAGASAKI TO YEDO.

IN the spring of 1861, returning from a visit to China, Sir Rutherford Alcock, on reaching Nagasaki, determined to make the journey from that place overland to Yedo, in the company of M. de Wit, the Dutch Minister. The English consul and an artist also joined the party, making five Europeans. The Japanese officials did not endeavor to prevent them from undertaking the journey, which had previously been made every four years by the Dutch Governor of Desima; but they did their best, although in vain, to retain the old charges and restrictions. The Dutch, it seemed, had always paid £4,000 as the expenses of the journey, which was so disproportioned to its actual cost that the two ministers determined to avoid the extortion by paying, themselves, all necessary expenses as they went along, — which amounted in the end to only £500. It was only after a great deal of trouble and delay that they succeeded in carrying their point.

The party finally left Nagasaki on the first of June, attended by a long retinue of *yaconins*, or guards, grooms, interpreters, and servants. The rain was pouring in torrents, and the commencement of the journey was as uncomfortable as it could well be. After leaving the last tea-houses in the suburbs of the city, the fields of grain and rice bordered the road, the former already ripened, while men and women, up to their knees in liquid mud, were busy in planting the latter. Sweet potatoes grew on terraces, supported by walls built along the faces of the hills; the hedges were overrun with honeysuckles and azaleas, while the pine, palm, bamboo, and cryptomeria grew side by side. The soil, although not naturally very fertile, was made, by careful cultivation, to yield a large return for labor.

The island of Kiusin, through which the travellers journeyed northward, toward the Straits of Simonoseki, which separate it from Nipon, is one of the three largest Japanese islands. "During this nine days' journey," says Sir Rutherford, "there was a combination of every kind of scenery. Well-cultivated valleys, winding among the hills, were graced with terraces stretching far up toward their summits, wherever a scanty soil could be found or *carried*, with a favorable aspect for the crops. We traversed some wild-looking passes, too, where hill and rock seemed tumbled in chaotic confusion from their volcanic beds. Frequent glimpses were caught of the sea-coast and bays, from which the road seldom strays very far inland. Pretty hamlets and clumps of fine trees were rarely wanting; and if the villages looked poor, and the peasant's home (bare of furniture at all times) more than usually void of comfort, yet all the people looked as if they had not only a roof to cover them, but rice to eat, which is more than can always be said of our populations in Europe. As groups of women and children crowded around the doors of the cottages, the whole interior of which the eye could easily take in at a glance, it would sometimes appear a problem how so many living beings could find sleeping room, or what provision there could be for the commonest requirements of decency, much less comfort. They must of necessity herd together very much like cattle; but neither is that, unfortunately, peculiar to Japan.

"At Urisino in the morning, and Takeiwa in the evening of the third day, we found some hot sulphur baths. The first we visited was open to the street, with merely a shed roof to shelter the bathers from the sun. As we approached, an elderly matron stepped out on the margin, leaving half a dozen of the other sex behind her to continue their soaking process. The freedom of the lady from all self-consciousness or embarrassment was perfect of its kind. The springs are close to the bank of a river, shaded by some noble trees; and the scene is both lively and picturesque, with groups of votaries, nude and undraped, crowding around the various reservoirs, and enjoying alternately the medicinal virtues of the waters and the cool shade of the trees."

On the third day the party passed a coal mine, belonging to the Prince of Fizen. It lay within a hundred yards of the main road, and a cross road led directly to it, but the way was stopped by a newly-erected barrier of bamboo. The English and Dutch Ministers, wishing to make a nearer inspection, passed this barrier, in spite of the outcries and protestations of the guards, who made every effort short of personal violence, to prevent them. There was simply a horizontal shaft into the side of the hill, with some heaps of inferior coal about its mouth. This appears to be the coal which is brought to Nagasaki, and sold to foreign steamers. The Prince of Fizen, it is said, ordered through the Dutch a steam-engine to aid in the better working of his mines; but, after it arrived and was conveyed to the spot, he changed his mind, declaring that it would take the bread out of his workmen's mouths. The attempt of the foreign ministers to examine the mines, was reported at Yedo afterwards, with many exaggerations, and made the subject of a complaint.

"On our way to Uzino, on the seventh day," says Sir Rutherford, "we passed through many scenes worthy of the artist's pencil; indeed, the number of tempting pictures was truly tantalizing, since it was clearly impossible to take even the slightest sketch of all. A little wayside shrine, embosomed in trees, was approached over a ravine, across which nature or art had flung a great boulder of granite. The scene, with a group of Japanese seated in the foreground, proved altogether irresistible. Again as we descended through a rocky pass into the valley below, and caught the first glimpse of the cultivated fields and terraced hills, with another range of mountains towering beyond, picturesque Japanese figures filling up the foreground, it was difficult to pass and take no note.

"On the eighth day, our way to Koyonoski lay chiefly along the banks of a river, on a high causeway raised some twenty feet above the level of the water. We passed several depots of coal, evidently placed there for embarkation, in some large flat-bottomed boats, a novel sight on the sand-choked rivers of Japan, — certainly in Kiusiu, where boats are to be seen only as exceptions. Kokura, the fortified capital of the province of Bouzen, and one of the keys to the strait between Kiusiu and Nipon, we reached early next morning, fortunately, for the sun beat hot upon our heads and shoulders long before ten o'clock. The roads were sheets of mud, and in places all but impassable with the heavy rains that had recently fallen; and, though the scenery was as beautiful as ever, it was difficult under such conditions to enjoy it. Pleasant country houses, each surrounded by its garden and clumps of trees or orchards, line the road which leads to the provincial capital, for more than a mile. It was holiday time, and all the inhabitants were at their windows, dressed in their best, or grouped on the doorsteps to watch the *cortege* pass.

"The entrance of Kokura is by a gateway, guarded by a considerable force of armed retainers. The walls were high, and seemed well capable of defense against anything but artillery. After a short halt, we embarked on board a junk, in the state cabin of which we had only the choice of squatting, or lying down between the ceiling and the floor. At the opposite side of the Straits, after a two hours' pull, we found H. M. S. *Ringdove* waiting our arrival, and we left the shores of Kiusiu, not sorry to have ended this much of our journey; for, despite all the attractions, novelty, and great beauty could lend, it was both fatiguing and tedious. Some seven or eight leagues a day on miserable ponies, led at a snail's pace over indifferent roads when at their best, and at this season often little better

SIMONOSEKI

than a series of pitfalls, was rather trying to the patience. We had traversed the territories of several daimios; of the princes of Omonra, Fizen, Secousin, and Izen; and from all I had seen, I drew the conclusion, that although the fertility of the soil is great, and turned to the best account by a plentiful supply of the cheapest labor, yet little superfluity is left to those who have to live by the cultivation of the land."

The party arrived at Simonoséki, the town on the Nipon shore of the strait, on the ninth day after leaving Nagasaki. At this port they decided to embark for Hiogo, at the farther end of the *Suonada*, or Inland Sea, instead of taking the rugged land-route along the sea-coast, which it would have required nearly three weeks to traverse. The distance from Simonoséki to Hiogo, which is near the large city of Osacca, is about two hundred and fifty miles by water.

Simonoséki is a town of about ten thousand inhabitants, extending in one straggling street for a mile and a half along the shore. The dwellings are mostly of wood, but the warehouses for goods are covered with a sort of white cement, or stucco, which is said to be fire-proof. Sugar, rice, iron, and oil, are the principal articles which are exported in junks to other parts of Japan. Among the curiosities of the place are two swords, said to have belonged to the Emperor Taikosama, and an ancient temple, in which there is a picture, three hundred years old, representing a famous sea-fight of one of the Japanese civil wars.

The party embarked in three large native junks, which were taken in tow by the British steamer, and were carried smoothly and slowly along through the

Inland Sea, lying at anchor every night. The shores of the surrounding islands are so lofty, that the water, protected from the severe storms and swells of the Pacific, resembles rather that of an inland lake. The villages along the shores are mostly poor fishing hamlets, with a barren country around them. The scenery of the voyage, nevertheless, from the height and variety of form of the mountain isles, is very beautiful.

At noon on the fourth day, the junks arrived at Hiogo, which is a town of about twenty thousands inhabitants, pleasantly situated along the edge of a sandy shore, with a range of wooded hills and mountains rising with a gentle slope behind. It is the shipping port of the great city of Osacca, which lies upon a river, some thirty miles inland. The harbor of Hiogo (or of Osacca, as it is sometimes called) is one of the best in Japan, hence the opening of this port to foreign commerce, with the condition of free access to the greater city, was a very important concession. Nevertheless, on this first visit, the shops were closed and the streets deserted, until the protestations of the ministers forced the Japanese officials to remove the restriction.

At Hiogo, other difficulties awaited the party. One of the Governors of Foreign Affairs had been sent from Yedo expressly to dissuade the ministers from continuing their journey by land. He declared that the country was in a disturbed state; that *lonins*, or bravos, were known to be ranging abroad, and that there was a temporary trouble between the Tycoon and the Mikado. It seemed to the ministers, however, that the main object of the mission was to prevent them from going to Miako, the capital of the Mikado,

ENTRANCE TO THE HARBOR OF HIOGO

and the ancient capital of Japan; for, when they had offered to give up this part of their plan, no serious objection was made to the overland journey to Yedo. From the attacks which were made on the foreign legations, shortly afterwards, it is possible that the ministers actually incurred a greater danger than they suspected at the time.

The distance from Hiogo to Osacca by land is about thirty miles. Nearly the whole way lies through the slopes and valleys intervening between the sea and the mountain range, trending inland. There are a great many rivers to be crossed; some over plank bridges almost too fragile for horses; others in boats, and others must be forded. The plain, which is sandy, is devoted to the cultivation of grain, cotton, and beans. The city of Osacca is first seen at the distance of a league, with the Tycoon's castle on a wooded eminence, commanding a view of the river. This is the ancient temple which Nobu Nanga took from the Buddhists, and which became the residence of Taikosama's son during the reign of Iyeyas. Sir Rutherford Alcock gives the following description of his arrival at Osacca:—

" We were nearly an hour in traversing the suburbs of this vast city, before we seemed to gain the great thoroughfare, filled to overflowing with an immense, but very orderly crowd. There was pushing and squeezing, and from time to time a desperate descent was made by the police on some luckless wights in the front rank. Blows on the bare head were dealt furiously on all; but the weapon was a fan, and although in their hands a very effective one, it could hardly do much mischief. We came at last to the main river, spanned by a bridge three hundred yards long, well and solidly built, below which there is an island, covered with houses, in the midst of the stream, something like the island of St. Louis in the Seine. Not a trace of hostile feeling was to be seen anywhere, though the curiosity was great to see the foreign ministers. Here, indeed, as might be noticed at a glance, was a vast population, with whom trade was the chief occupation; and at every step evidences of the greatest activity were visible. Piled up near the bridge I noticed glazed tiles for drains, and large earthen jars for coffins — the Japanese being buried as he lives, with his heels tucked up under him in a sitting posture, — an arrangement which has at least the advantage of saving space in the cemeteries, still further economized by burning the bodies of the poorer classes, and merely burying their ashes in a jar of small dimensions. The Japanese have some strange superstitions about either sleeping or being buried with the head to the north. In every sleeping-room at the resting-places, we found the points of the compass marked on the ceiling; and my Japanese servant would on no account let my bed be made up in any but the right direction."

The travellers were lodged in a large temple, with some pretensions to architectural beauty. The first day they devoted to shopping and the theatre, reserving a second day to be spent in traversing the city by water, as in Venice — by means of the river-arms which divide it, — and in visiting the larger temples and the Tycoon's castle. They visited some silk shops so large that from fifty to one hundred attendants were constantly employed. Bronzes were also very beautiful and cheap; but lacquer-ware was astonishingly dear, and from forty to fifty dollars apiece were demanded for small, ugly, pug-nosed, goggle-eyed dogs. By slipping away from their Japanese attendants, the travellers succeeded in obtaining some very rare and beautiful specimens of porcelain. As soon as the attendants rejoined them, the price of every article immediately advanced fifty per cent.

The day devoted to the exploration of the city by water was one of great interest. There are thirteen rivers and canals, and at least a hundred bridges, many of them of enormous width and costly structure, span these streams in all directions. The banks of the main river are lined for two or three miles with the residences of daimios, with broad flights of granite steps descending to the water's edge. Thousands of boats, filled with merchandise or passengers, covered the broad surface of the waters; and every bridge was crowded to an alarming extent by the population, eager to see the foreigners. Later in the day the latter made an effort to visit some of the older and more celebrated temples; but they were foiled by the cunning of the Japanese attendants, who, after dragging them about for an hour or two in the hot sun, took them finally to some ruined walls. In the same manner they were prevented from seeing the Tycoon's castle. The friendly and confiding manner of the inhabitants toward them contrasted strongly with the jealousy and meddlesome interference of the officials, and they were satisfied that the opposition to intercourse with foreigners in Japan is not founded on anything in the character of the people.

Leaving for Yedo on the 19th of June, they passed many large villages on the plain around Osacca. The population, for the first time during the journey, was noisy and troublesome, crying out, " Chinese hucksters ! " as they passed through, — but there was good reason for suspicion that the officers of the escort, who had meant to stay another day in the city, had commanded this reception, as a piece of spite. Beyond the plain, there is a mountain range, about four thousand feet in height, which the road crosses into a beautiful valley beyond. Here the unfriendly manifestations ceased : the Tokaido, or high road, had been swept clean for the passage of some native princes, and small boys, with brooms, ran along in advance of the foreign ministers, shouting, " Down on your knees ! " to all the natives they met.

On the third day the road entered a very picturesque country. " We rode through defiles of mountains, amidst a very chaos of hills and ravines, the former tumbled wildly together, looking like a troubled sea of billows suddenly petrified. It must have been the theatre of some long extinct volcanic action ; for miles, half-filled craters were the leading feature. This was the circuitous route adopted, in order to leave Miako to the left, compelling us to take a cross-road only some five or six feet in width, winding around the bases of the hills."

The Japanese officials accompanying the party insisted on halting for the night at a little village named Saki, instead of the larger town of Nieno, which had

DAIMIOS.

been selected in advance as the resting-place. They asserted that the houses for travellers were undergoing repair, and the change of programme was accompanied with so much inconvenience to themselves, that the ministers finally agreed to it. But, on reaching Nieno, the following morning, they were surprised to find it a stately, well-built place, the houses all in perfect order, but every door and window hermetically closed, and not a living face to be seen. Even the residence of the Daimio — the same Toda-Idzu-no-Kami, who was one of the first commissioners to meet Commodore Perry at Gori-hama in 1853 — was masked by screens of cotton cloth. It was, of course, impossible to obtain from the Japanese any explanation of this extraordinary proceeding; but it must be attributed to an assertion of defiant independence of the Tycoon's authority, on the part of the Prince of Idzu. This disposition, on the part of those princes who are hostile to foreign intercourse, to disregard the treaties made by the government, has since been more strikingly illustrated in the case of the Prince of Satsuma, and the punishment which he received from the English forces in consequence.

"Our way lay for many days," the author continues, "through mountain scenery and fertile valleys, the hills generally clothed to the very summit with trees, chiefly of the pine family. The same sandy character of the soil, and the formation of the hills already noticed, continued until we approached within sight of Fusi-yama, when it was exchanged for the dark rich mould which alone is to be seen within a hundred miles of Yedo. On the fourth day we had struck into the ordinary route, and had the advantage of the fine sanded roads and park-like avenues of the Tokaido. And now each day we met one or more *corteges* of daimios coming from the capital. As a general rule we had nothing to complain of; if some of the principal officers and armed retainers scowled at us, and seemed to think our presence on the high roads an offense, the greater number passed on their way, as we did on ours, without any manifestation of feeling or opinion. In one case only, I was amused by a somewhat characteristic trait. Mr. De Wit and I were riding abreast and without any escort, having left them far behind, when, seeing a rather large *cortege* filling up the road as we turned an angle, we drew to one side and went in single file. No sooner did the leading officer observe the movement than he instantly began to swagger, and motioned all the train to spread themselves over the whole road; so that all we gained by our consideration and courtesy was to run the risk of being pushed into the ditch by an insolent subordinate. Thus it is ever in the East. To yield the wall is a sign of weakness; to yield to anything spontaneously, is to provoke oppression; and they who, from courtesy, step aside, are fortunate if they do not get trampled down for cowards and fools.

"As we advanced through the country, both men and women were busily employed in planting out their rice. This was the first time I had seen any but isolated cases of women being engaged in field labor in Japan; for the Japanese appear to me to be honorably distinguished among nations of a higher civilization, in that they leave their women to the lighter work of the house, and perform themselves the harder out-door labor. Indeed, I was at first in some doubt here, for it was by no means easy to distinguish the women from the men at a little distance. To guard the legs probably from leeches, as they paddled in the mud, they all wore gaiters up to the knees and short cotton trousers. When the neck was covered, there was no very distinguishing difference between the sexes, as the men never have any hair about the face. The wheat in Japan never appears to be sown broadcast. All that I have seen has been drilled and planted in rows, much as the rice is, a few stalks together. Labor is cheap, and it is to be presumed they find this the more profitable way.

"As we approached Mia, on the bay of Owari, we passed another great castle. And yet this term is very likely, I fear, to mislead the reader. What constitutes a daimio's castle, then, in Japan, is first a moat surrounded by a wall, generally built of mud intersected with layers of tiles, and plastered over; sometimes with parapets, and loopholed for musketry; a large gateway, with massive overhanging roof; a straggling group of ignoble-looking lath and plaster houses inside, rarely more than one story high, and sometimes, if the owner is a daimio of very great pretensions, his walls will be flanked with turrets. In his grounds, something like a two or three storied pagoda will rise above the dead level of the other roofs, and look picturesque through the clumps of fine timber, with which the grounds of the owners are always graced, whatever else may be wanting."

The travellers were six hours in crossing the bay of Owari, to reach Mia, where the Tokaido recommences, on the opposite side, the distance being about twenty miles. From this place to the next large town of Ocasaki, the road led through a beautiful open country, with mountains on the horizon. Villages and towns follow in quick succession; and rarely at a greater interval than one or two leagues at farthest, along the whole route from Nagasaki to Yedo. At a place called Arai, there was another bay to cross, a distance of about three miles; but a broad canal, for the passage of boats, was cut through the shallows and sand bars.

More than half the distance between Osacca and Yedo had now been traversed, and the annoying interference of the Japanese authorities began to diminish. Immediately after leaving Hamamatz, the half-way town, the travellers were obliged to make their way across a plain, traversed in all directions by floods and water-courses, swelled by the rains, which had broken the bridges and damaged all the roads. One of the villages through which they passed was devoted entirely to the plaiting of straw-shoes. At another place, called Cakengawa, the people are celebrated for weaving a kind of linen from the bark of a creeper. Rain coats are made of the same bark, unwoven, and only slightly plaited, and they are highly esteemed as both light and impervious.

After crossing another high range of mountains, with very wild and grand scenery, the road descended to the river Oigawa, which was so swollen by rain that the party was obliged to wait until the next morning before they were able to cross. The ministers were carried across in the *norimons*, or native palanquins of Japan, carried upon the shoulders of the ferrymen. The poorer natives, men and women, bestride the latters' shoulders, holding their garments up to the waist while crossing the deeper parts.

From the banks of this river the first view of Fusi-yama, on this journey, was obtained. This was a welcome proof to the weary travellers that the journey was drawing to an end; and here, in fact, Sir Rutherford Alcock's journey terminates. There were still three days of travel before reaching the old road to the capital, taken on making the trip to the summit of Fusi-yama, the previous year, and the great Hakoni range was to be crossed; but all was safely accomplished, and on the thirty-second day after leaving Nagasaki, the party reached the small foreign settlement at Kanagawa.

Sir Rutherford Alcock returned to the British Legation at Yedo on the 4th of July, and on the night of the 5th the murderous attack was made, in which Mr. Oliphant, the Secretary of Legation, and Mr. Morrison, British Consul at Nagasaki, were severely wounded. The Japanese guard of one hundred and fifty persons was conveniently absent or asleep, and the escape of all the foreigners from a bloody death could only be attributed to the haste or confusion of the assassins. The attack was traced to the hostility of one of the native princes, and the murder of Mr. Huesken, Interpreter of the American Legation, in the streets of Yedo, five months previously, must be ascribed to the same source.

CHAPTER VI.

M. HUMBERT'S VOYAGE FROM NAGASAKI TO YEDO.

M. AIMÉ HUMBERT, appointed by the Swiss Government in 1862 an Envoy Extraordinary for the purpose of making a commercial treaty with Japan, remained some years in the latter country, and employed his leisure time to excellent purpose in studying the history, the laws, manners and customs of the Japanese. His work, published in 1870, in two large quarto volumes, with nearly five hundred admirable illustrations, mostly from photographs taken on the spot, is much the most careful and thorough which has yet appeared. His travels in the interior were limited, it is true, by political disturbances; but his chief point of observation was Yedo, where the natives of all parts of the empire may be studied, nearly as well as in their separate provinces, and where all the peculiar customs of the race are displayed on the largest scale.

Reaching Nagasaki in April, 1863, M. Humbert was hospitably received by the Dutch agent, M. de Wit, and took up his residence, temporarily, on the island of Desima. He found that the Japanese city of Nagasaki was now entirely free to Europeans, who were permitted to wander through its streets at their pleasure. He was charmed with the situation of the town, and the beauty of its environs. The native place contains, at present, about eighty thousand inhabitants. The houses are all built of wood, but there is a staircase of granite connecting the lower city with the upper, and a massive stone bridge across the principal of the mountain torrents which divide the streets. Preparations were already made for the construction of a foreign quarter upon the mainland, opposite the island of Desima, which is much too small for the necessities of the commerce of all nations.

After a stay of twelve days, M. Humbert took passage on the Dutch frigate *Koopman* for the Bay of Yedo, by way of the Suonada, or Inner Sea. The course was at first westward, making for the Strait of Specx, between Firando and Kiusiu. The mountainous coasts of the latter island, like rocky fortresses, defended by lines of breakers, give no indication of the fertility of the interior. Barren and uninhabited, they seem to repel all who would dare to land upon them. The currents on this part of the coast are so strong and uncertain, that the frigate was compelled to anchor for the night among a crowd of Japanese junks, under the lee of Firando.

The next day, the western coast of Kiusiu was thronged with quantities of fishing-boats and coasting junks. There are good harbors and large maritime towns on this part of the island. The rocks which stud the shores are the resorts of immense numbers of wild geese and ducks, which the Japanese have not yet learned to eat. Domestic fowls, however, are plentiful everywhere, and the common people will always give a hen in exchange for an empty bottle. In the markets of Yedo, the latter article is always in demand, and, curiously enough, a double price is willingly paid for a bottle which has a brilliant label, no matter of what kind.

The frigate anchored, the second evening, in the Straits of Van der Capellen, in front of the town of Simonoséki. The water, next morning, was covered with native boats, filled with fishermen, traders, or the families of respectable citizens, eager for a nearer view of the strange vessel. But, after a visit from some of the authorities, the voyage was resumed. The day, however, was foggy, and the Japanese pilots on board kept the centre of the strait until they reached the broader waters of the Inner Sea. When the weather became clear, the multitude of islands always in sight, with their constantly changing forms, gave a new interest to the voyage. Some were arid, of a brown or black tint, shooting up like cones, pyramids, or jagged fangs, out of the water; others were fertile, their sides laboriously wrought into terraces for grain and vegetables, with little villages of farmers and fishermen in the sheltered coves.

In entering the basin of Bingo, the large town of Imabari, on the coast of the island of Sikok, came into view. On a sandy bar, stretching from one of the suburbs, there appeared to be a grand fair, or market, judging from the crowds of people. Beyond the town were fertile plains, swelling into hills in the distance, where mountain-peaks, from three to five thousand feet in height, closed the view. Around Imabari, there were some low batteries, from which flags were flying, groups of soldiers stood upon the ramparts. Shortly afterwards, a large Japanese steamer passed the frigate.

The pilots declared that it belonged to the Prince of Tosa, one of the eighteen Chief Daimios of the empire, whose possessions, in the southern part of Sikok, yield him an annual revenue of $750,000. He was perhaps returning home from a conference of the "feudal party," making convenient use of the very improvements which he was endeavoring to banish from Japan!

The second night after leaving Simonoséki, was passed in one of those broader basins of the Inner Sea, called the Arimanada. It is almost completely closed, on the east, by the large island of Awadsi, which shuts out the ocean for a space of thirty miles, between Sikok and Nipon. This island was the fabled residence of the earlier gods, the cradle of the national mythology of the Japanese. The lowlands at its northern extremity are covered with a superb vegetation; toward the south it rises gradually into hills, still beautifully cultivated, and is finally crowned by a mountain range.

The steamers which traverse the Inner Sea, generally take the northern passage, between Awadsi and Nipon, partly in order to touch at Hiogo, and partly because the southern passage, between Awadsi and Sikok, is considered dangerous for vessels of deep draught. The captain of the frigate, nevertheless, determined to try the latter. Leaving Awadsi on the left, he steered down the narrowing strait, between finely cultivated shores, bordered with rocky islets, crowned with pine-trees. The water in front presented the appearance of a bar of breakers; yet the weather was calm, and the open ocean, in the distance, did not show a speck of foam. It was evident that the agitation of the water was occasioned solely by the violence of conflicting currents. Millions of sea-birds filled the air, drifting around the rocks like clouds, or dashing down to the sea with continual cries. There were many fishing-boats in the calmer channels between the islands, or the coves of the shores, but none of them ventured into the raging flood which filled the strait. The breadth of the main channel was estimated at eight hundred yards, with a length of nearly two miles.

After passing safely through, the frigate entered a broad strait beyond, where the swells of the Pacific were already felt. The Inner Sea was left behind, and in leaving it, M. Humbert says, after expatiating on the beauty of its scenery: " However, setting aside the question of the picturesque, which, I grant, is not the essential element of our relations with the extreme East, I hope that, sooner or later, there will be formed in Japan a chain of Western colonies, peaceably developing the natural and commercial resources of that admirable country, along a line indicated by Yokohama, Hiogo, Simonoséki, and Nagasaki. They would be united by regular steam communication. The steamships of America, as well as those of China, would nourish the relations of both worlds with the great archipelago of the Pacific. Europeans, weary of a tropical climate, or of the burdens of business in China, would then come to seek a pure and bracing air, and a season of repose, on the shores of the Japanese Mediterranean. How many families established in China, how many European women with their children, would be happy to exchange the trying summer months for a refuge worthy the most beautiful regions of Italy, and yet so near their present residence!"

After having doubled the cape of Idsoumo, the southern promontory of Nipon, the frigate took advantage of the *Kuro-siwo*, or Asiatic gulf stream, which flows northward past the eastern shores of Japan, at the rate of thirty-five to forty miles per day. Its maximum temperature there is about 85°. It is the same warm current which carries fog and rain to Alaska, and, according to some modern geographers, opens a practicable route, through Behring's Straits, to the North Pole. After a day of tranquil navigation they made, at sunrise, the promontory of Idzu, in a bight of which is the town of Simoda, one of the ports opened to American vessels in 1854. After the great earthquake, the following year, in which the Russian frigate *Diana* was dashed to pieces, and which so changed the harbor as to injure its value for commerce, Simoda was given up, and the more important town of Kanagawa, near Yedo, substituted for it, in the American treaty of 1858.

When the outer bay of Sagami had been passed, and the frigate entered the broad strait of Uraga, which opens into the Bay of Yedo, M. Humbert thus recalls the memorable event of ten years before: "On the chart which they have made of the Bay of Yedo, the Americans have consecrated the souvenirs of their glorious enterprise by a series of denominations of places, which the geographers and navigators have already ratified. In front of the town of Uraga is *Reception Bay*, and beyond it, the bar which forms

Cape Kamisaki is *Rubicon Point;* the bight which opens on the left is *Susquehanna Bay;* above its limpid waters rise *Perry Island,* and *Webster Island;* on the right, from the other shore, extends *Cape Saratoga;* and this side of Yokohama *Mississippi Bay* stretches to the end of *Treaty Point.* It is thus that on these waters and along these shores of one of the most charming countries of the world, unknown until our day, the names of the New World and of our cosmopolitan age are wedded to the names of more than twenty centuries of the Empire of the Rising Sun."

As they passed up the bay, the solitary cone of Fusi-yama came out in all its snowy splendor; then, doubling Treaty Point, the harbor of Yokohama suddenly opened, with its foreign shipping, its white foreign houses, and consular residences, with the flags of their respective nations.

And not quite ten years had elapsed, since the first foreign vessels had ever ploughed those waters — since Commodore Perry, coming after the failures of two centuries, knocked loudly at the door of the **great empire,** and it was opened to him!

CHAPTER VII.

RESIDENCE AT YOKOHAMA.

M. HUMBERT first took up his residence in the house of the Dutch Consul-general, in the Japanese quarter of Yokohama, which is there known under the name of Benten. The house was built by the Japanese, and was an attempt to combine native and European ideas, in its architecture and arrangement. It was a parallelogram, partly of brick and partly of wood, with a spacious veranda on the eastern, western, and northern sides. All the occupied rooms opened upon this veranda by double glass doors, which took the place of windows. The greater part of the main edifice was used for store-rooms, baths, stables, and the residence of the native servants, of whom there were a large number. In the rear there was a garden, surrounded with palisades, and with a porter's lodge.

The porter was a respectable, married Japanese, who exercised a sort of patriarchal authority over the other domestics. His lodge, where there were always a tea-machine, a little furnace, pipes and tobacco, was the rendezvous of a crowd of native idlers and gossips; but his services, nevertheless, were always rendered punctually and correctly. He was not only required to keep a general watch, to open or close the doors which he had in charge, but also to sound the hours of day and night by striking with a mallet upon a gong, and to announce in the same way the character of the visitor — one stroke signifying a merchant or plain citizen, two strokes an officer, or interpreter, three a consul or Japanese governor, and four a minister or admiral. He was also responsible for the night-watch, which must visit every part of the building half hourly during the night.

Along the southern palisade were the stables and laundry, and opposite to them the residences of the *bettos*, or grooms. Every horse in Japan has his separate betto, who always accompanies him when ridden out, running in advance or at the side of the horseman. These robust fellows form, in Japan, a corporation or guild, which has its own separate government, the chief officer of which enjoys the right of wearing a sword. They are of medium stature, but strong and well proportioned. Their lives are spent in a state of almost complete nudity; though they generally wear sandals, a loin-cloth, and a short jacket when accompanying their masters abroad.

M. Humbert had as valet a little Japanese boy, by the name of Tô. He was a fellow of quick intelligence, but with an air of gravity and prudence much beyond his years. "It was from Tô," says the minister, "that I took my first Japanese lesson. He gave me the key to conversation in three words, and the philosophical character of the method he employed will at once be appreciated. The operations of the mind resolve themselves into three forms — doubt, negation and affirmation. As soon as one knows how to express

JAPANESE BÉTOS.

these three operations, the rest is only a matter of the Vocabulary, — a charging of the memory with a certain number of the usual words. Thus we will commence with doubt, and say in Japanese, *Arimaska?* which signifies, 'Is there?' Then we pass to negation, *Arimasi*, 'There is not,' and finish with *Arimas*, 'There is.' After that, the Vocabulary will furnish us with the words which we most need, as *Nipon*, Japan, Japanese; *chi*, fire; *cha*, tea; *ma*, a horse; *mizu*, water, etc. Add a little mimicry, and we shall be able to comprehend many things without the aid of an interpreter. Thus coming home after a long ride, I order Tô to bring me tea: '*Cha arimaska?*' He answers, '*Arimas*,' and soon the refreshing beverage is on my table. By the same process, I tell him to put the water on the fire, or in the tea, to call the betto and have the horse saddled, etc."

That part of Yokohama which is called Benten, takes its name from a goddess of the sea, who is still adored on a neighboring island. Before the arrival of foreigners, this sacred spot was surrounded only by a settlement of fishers and farmers, separated by a marsh from the unimportant village of Yokohama. At present the quays, streets, and substantial modern buildings have covered all the space from Treaty Point to the small river which divided the two original villages. The streets of Benten have not yet been materially changed: they are connected with the new portion by a bridge, almost concealed from view by the trees and bamboo thickets which shade it. Another bridge, on the western side, leads to the grove in which stands the temple of the goddess, with the residence of the officiating priests. In the neighborhood there is a restaurant, or tea-house, which also furnishes *saki*, the intoxicating liquor distilled from rice, fruits, fish, and wheaten cakes. The regiment of soldiers, which performs the office of a government guard, is also quartered in this part of the town.

At first the native population seemed somewhat reserved, not with any evidence of unfriendly feeling, but apparently waiting until the strangers should make the first advances. "Little by little," says M. Humbert, "neighborly relations were established between our residence and the quarter of the *yakounins* (guards). In Japan, as elsewhere, little presents create friendly feelings. Some packages of white sugar and Java coffee, sent to those families where we learned that there were recent births, or invalids, were gratefully received.

"One day, when I was entirely alone, between four and five in the afternoon, the porter announced to me the arrival of a deputation of native ladies, and asked whether they should be received. These ladies had received from their husbands permission to return their thanks for the presents, but they also wished to examine our European mode of living. I ordered the porter to admit them, and took upon myself the duty of receiving them with all due honor.

"I soon heard the sound of wooden shoes on the gravel of the garden-alleys, and saw, at the foot of the steps leading to the veranda, a group of smiling faces, among whom were four married women, two marriageable girls, and children of various ages. The first could be distinguished by the plainness of their toi-

JAPANESE LADIES GOING TO PAY A VISIT

lets, having no ornaments in their hair, nothing fine or brilliantly colored in their clothing, no rouge on the face, but the teeth black as ebony, in accordance with Japanese usage; the young girls, on the contrary, increase the natural whiteness of the teeth by a coat of carmine on the lips, rouge their cheeks, braid bands of scarlet crape among their black hair, and wear a broad girdle of brilliant colors. As to the children, their costume consisted of gay plaid robes and girdles; their heads were shaved, but, according to age or sex, several tufts of greater or less length were left, some loose, some bound together in a sort of *chignon*.

"After the usual salutations and bows, the orators of the deputation, — for there were two or three who spoke at once, — made me many handsome compliments in Japanese, to which I replied in French, inviting them to enter the *salon*. Certainly I had been understood; for I heard expressions of thanks which I had already learned; and yet, instead of ascending the steps, they appeared to ask some further, unintelligible explanation. Finally the graceful company perceived my ignorance; adding gesture to words, they asked: 'Shall we take off our shoes in the garden, or will it answer to do so on the veranda?' I decided in favor of the latter; whereupon they mounted the steps, took off and arranged their sandals, and joyously trod the carpets of the *salon*, the children with bare feet, the grown persons with cotton stockings, divided at the end by a *thumb* for the great toe.

"Their first impression was a naïve admiration of what they saw, followed immediately by a general hilarity, for the tall pier-glasses, descending to the floor, reflected and repeated their forms, from head to foot, behind as well as in front. While the younger visitors continued to contemplate this phenomenon, so new and attractive to them, the married women asked me to explain the meaning of the pictures on the walls. I stated that they represented the Tycoon of Holland and wife, together with several great daimios of the reigning family. They respectfully bowed; but one of them, whose curiosity was not satisfied, timidly expressed the opinion that the portrait of the *betto* of his Dutch Majesty had been included in the royal company. I did not enlighten her, for she could never have comprehended the noble fashion of representing a prince on foot, beside his saddle-horse, and even holding the bridle, like a Japanese groom! Others, after having carefully examined the velvet of the chairs and sofas, came to me for the decision of a question which had arisen among them, concerning the use of those pieces of furniture. They agreed that the chairs were made to be sat upon; but the sofas? Did we not crouch upon them, with crossed legs, when the meals were served? They heartily commiserated the ladies and gentlemen of the West, who were obliged to use such an inconvenient piece of furniture, always sitting with their feet painfully resting on the floor.

"My bedroom, opening from the *salon*, was next invaded. I cannot describe all the subjects of astonishment discovered by the curious troop. Being Japanese, they were none the less daughters of Eve; and the forbidden fruit which tempted them the most was an assortment of uniform buttons with the Swiss cross upon them, according to the military usage of my country. I was obliged to give them a few, although it was impossible to conjecture what use they would make of them, since all Japanese garments, male or female, are simply bound with silk cords. The gift of some articles of Parisian perfumery was well appreciated; but I could not make them understand the merits of *eau de Cologne*, for the cambric handkerchief is unknown to Japanese ladies. They informed me that the poorest girl would never degrade herself by carrying in her pocket an article with which she had wiped her nose. The little squares of paper which they carry for the purpose are not likely, therefore, to be easily supplanted.

"To restore the balance, I exhibited to them a case containing an assortment of sewing-thread, pins, and needles, and asked them to make use of it. They were unanimous in recognizing the imperfection of all their native implements for sewing. The needle by no means occupies the same place in their native society as in our family circles at home. Sewing, for example, is never seen during the visits and the long gossips of the Japanese women; even as men, in Europe, have recourse to the cigar, they employ only the pipe, to season their hours of conversation. I gave to the children some small pictures of Swiss landscapes and costumes, and showed to the grown persons an album of family photographs, which they examined with an interest, an expression of feeling, truly touching."

M. Humbert unites with many American residents of Yokohama, in testifying to the kind and friendly character of the common people. The fishing population of Benten always accosted him with a pleasant greet-

JAPANESE CROSSING A MOUNTAIN GORGE.

themselves in swinging baskets over the most frightful depths.

The country around Yokohama is thoroughly cultivated, and covered with dwellings. The isolated houses are built near the roads, and even those which line the highway are usually entirely open, and free to light and air. In order to enjoy the fresh breezes, the inhabitants shove to the right and left the movable screens which inclose their dwellings, and thus completely expose their domestic arrangements to the view of those who pass. It is therefore not difficult to observe their manner of living, as well as the distinctive characteristics of the different classes of society. The conventional separation of the latter does not seem to depend on any important difference of blood or of habits. The families of the yakounin live in the same manner, and with the same domestic customs, as those of the peasants and mechanics; and, with the exception of a greater luxury in dress and meals, the households of the higher government officials are very similar.

The Japanese are of medium stature, and have scarcely the slightest resemblance to the Chinese, either in face, form, or complexion. The only European race which they sometimes suggest in their appearance, is the Portuguese. There is more difference in the relative height of the sexes than in Europe. According to the observations made by Dr. Mohnike, at Desima, the medium stature of the men is five Paris feet, one or two inches, and of the women, four feet, one to three inches. Men of six feet, however, are not uncommon. They all have straight, thick, jet black hair; the men lave beards, but the custom of shaving is universal. The color of their skin varies, according to the classes of society, from the dark, coppery-brown of the Malays to the dead-white or tawny of Southern Europe. The prevailing tint is a dark olive, which has no affinity to the yellow of the Chinese. Unlike the Europeans, their faces and hands are generally lighter colored than their bodies. Children, youths, and girls often have a fresh rosy color, with a red on their cheeks, like that of the fairer races. The women sometimes appear perfectly white; in fact, a uniform, dead white complexion is considered a sign of aristocratic blood. In two particulars, however, they are all unlike the Europeans, — in the peculiar slant of the eyes, and an ungraceful narrowness and flatness of the breast.

The national Japanese costume is the *kirimon*, a sort of open dressing-gown, which is made a little longer and fuller for the women than for the men. It is crossed in front, and held in its place by a girdle, for which the men use a silk scarf, and the women a broad band, highly ornamented, and fastened upon the back. They wear no linen, but bathe every day; the women, alone, sometimes have a chemise of red crape. In summer, the peasants, fishers, bettos, porters, and other laboring classes are nude, except a narrow girdle around the loins; and the bathing-houses of the people are as freely open to the public as their dwellings.

In winter, the common people wear a close fitting jacket and trousers of blue cotton cloth, under the *kirimon*, and the women one or more wadded mantles. The men of the better class, and the nobles, never go abroad without the jacket and trousers; the principal difference of costume between the classes is only in the material, the nobles alone having the right to wear silk. They only dress very richly when they go to court, or make visits of ceremony. All classes have the same covering for the feet, — cotton socks, and straw sandals, or wooden soles, fastened by a strap passing inside the great toe. When the roads are very muddy, they use pattens, very simply constructed of three pieces of wood. Every one, on entering his own, or a neighbor's house, leaves his sandals at the door.

CHAPTER VIII.

EXCURSION TO KAMAKURA.

DURING the Japanese summer, there is rarely a long succession of fine days. During the months of June and July, there is an alternation of sultry heats and furious rains, as in tropical countries. Thunderstorms generally arise in the direction of Fusi-yama, descend to the bay, and finally pass away to spend their greatest violence on the ocean; the islands are not often visited with the furious typhoons of the Chinese Sea.

During this season, M. Humbert, weary of his quiet life at Benten, and of nightly battles with the mosquitoes, projected in company with some of the other foreign residents, an excursion to the old city of Kamakura, the residence of the Tycoons before Iyeyas removed the capital to Yedo. It is situated on the seashore, at the head of the deep bay of Sagami, and not more than twenty miles in a direct line from Yokohama. After much consultation, the travellers, three in number, decided to go down the bay in a boat as far as the village of Kanasawa, whence it was but a land journey of five miles to Kamakura.

"It was nine o'clock in the evening when we embarked," M. Humbert writes. "Two Japanese sentinels on the shore, armed with a musket without bayonet, saluted us with a peaceable ' good evening!' From all the barques moored to the quay, arose, like a rhythmical moaning, the monotonous prayer of the fishermen to the supreme intercessor and patron of souls: 'Amida, have mercy upon us!' The efficacy of this prayer depends on the number of minutes uninterruptedly devoted to it, according to the direction of the bonzes, or priests.

"Our crew was composed of five boatmen, the constable, two valets, and a Chinese *comprador* (steward). They were all ready on the quarter-deck of the junk, leaving the cabin at our disposition. We arranged three sleeping-places out of sacks, boxes, and such coverings as we had brought with us, and then mounted to the deck to enjoy the night. The boatmen, who were obliged to row across that part of the harbor occupied by the fleet, stood on their feet, two on each side, leaning on their long, plunging oars, to which they gave a sort of rotary movement in rowing, like the Venetian gondoliers. The fifth stood upon the stern, and managed the rudder. The effect of this manner of rowing was like that of a screw-engine.

"Afterwards a light breeze having arisen, our boatmen drew in their oars and hoisted sail. We were soon on the open water, losing sight of the shores, and all place of embarkation; the sky was covered with floating vapors, and the moon gave but a misty light. But when we went below to sleep, we found, to our horror, that the mosquitoes were there before us. There was nothing to do but to return to the deck, order our Chinaman to prepare tea, and pass the rest of the night crouched around the fire in his brazier.

"In the early dawn, the boatmen hauled down the

sail and resumed their oars. We began to distinguish, on our right, a steep, picturesque promontory, clothed with beautiful groups of trees, and, directly in front of us, the domes of foliage which crown Webster Island. Skirting its shores, we entered by a narrow channel into the harbor of Kanasawa, passing a number of fishing boats which were silently pushing out to their day's labor. At the entrance of the port a little temple, surrounded with fruit trees, occupies the centre of a low island, connected with the market-place by a jetty; further, on a massive pile of rocks, overlooking some sacred buildings, there is a tea-house with an observatory commanding a panorama of the entire bay.

"The Japanese have a lively feeling for the beauty of their country. There is no picturesque point to which they do not call public attention, by building there a chapel, a tea-house, a pavilion, or some sort of an edifice inviting repose. Nowhere is the traveller so frequently invited to delay his journey, and relieve himself of fatigue under some hospitable roof, or cool shade, with a lovely landscape before his eyes.

"We entered an hostelry near the port. A spacious gallery, above the level of the street, was put at our disposal. Some planks laid upon trestles, two benches and empty boxes enable us to seat ourselves at table in the European manner. We breakfasted on our own provisions, to which the hostess added tea, saki, rice, fried fish, and soy. She was assisted by two young servant-girls. neatly dressed, and *coiffées* with even an air of elegance. Toward the close of our meal the children of the house timidly mounted the steps leading to our room; but, on my beckoning the youngest, he set

JAPANESE TEA HOUSE.

up a loud cry. I drew from my pocket some pictured labels which I was in the habit of carrying about with me, and very soon he came to beg one of me. Then followed his mother, the girls of the inn, and the women of the neighborhood, with their children. An old grandmother expressed a wish to taste some white sugar, for the raw brown sugar brought from Loo-Choo is the only kind known in Japan. We succeeded, finally, in making them understand that we needed rest; whereupon they withdrew as gently and noiselessly as if we were already slumbering.

"A sleeping-place was improvised by using a number of double screens, in order to divide the room into a number of separate retreats. I say separate, rather than inclosed, for the paper screens were not without holes; and after I was stretched upon the matting, with my head on a travelling-cushion, I more than once saw a curious eye sparkling through the apertures. Finally I slept, but not for a long time. The matting of these Japanese houses serves as a retreat for multitudes of those insects which Toepffer has designated by the name of 'domestic kangaroos.' My comrades had the same experience, and we very soon returned to the open gallery."

The day, which turned out to be rainy, was spent, perforce, in the tea-house. A dinner of fish, which the travellers were allowed to select from the tank in which they swam, was served by the hostess, with the usual rice-cakes, and a dessert of fruit. In the afternoon they had a visit from a female professor of music, a performer on the *samsin*, a rude stringed instrument, somewhat resembling a guitar. One of the company had a music-box, which played several French airs; and they were all astonished at the skill with which the Japanese musician caught them up and repeated them on her instrument.

After another uncomfortable night, the greater part of the company (some of whom had arrived by land), who had intended making an excursion to the remarkable volcanic island of Inosima, decided to return to Yokohama. M. Humbert and two others, with the constable, set out on foot for the old capital of Kamakura. "It was four o'clock in the morning," he writes, "when we left the tea-house. We traversed the deserted streets of Kanasawa in a southern direction, to the last of the chain of hills against which the village leans. There, some constructions of a peculiar style announce a seignorial residence. Strong walls surround and support garden terraces: a portal, formed of two pillars and a cross-piece of massive oak, covered with black varnish and adorned with ornaments of copper, gives access to a spacious court-yard. Therein we distinguish a guard-house and other buildings, behind which there are great trees, which give an antique character to the residence. I learned that it belongs to the prince Noné-kura Tango, whose annual revenue is about 160,000 francs.

"Further on, after having crossed a bridge over a rapid river flowing to the west, we approach that chain of wooded mountains which divides the peninsula of Sagami into two opposite slopes. Around us the soil is cultivated; fields of beans have replaced the wheat harvested in June; the rice still rolls in green waves, but already in head. The paths which lead through the fields are so narrow that there is only space to put one foot before the other. Even on the road we followed, two horses could scarcely go abreast: yet upon it, we encountered a singular obstacle. An old man and his wife had chosen it as an economical lodging-place for the night, and were sleeping upon two bamboo mats which were probably also their travelling cloaks. A little heap of smoking ashes indicated that they had made a fire of reeds to drive away the mosquitoes from their rural couch.

"Rising from the foot of the hills, the road winds among rocks of sandstone, sometimes sharply pointed, often pierced with grottoes in which we discover little idols, altars, or votive offerings. On the summit of the ridge there is a cabin of planks and mats, built against a wall of rock, and containing some benches, a hearth, and utensils for preparing tea and rice. At this early morning hour it is uninhabited, and its furniture is intrusted to the honesty of the public. The descent on the other side is rapid. A beautiful golden pheasant looks at us from the border of a grove; one of my companions cannot resist the temptation of discharging his revolver. But the bird, untouched, does not seem to be much concerned by the attempt; and only after some reflection, does he judge it prudent to remove to the top of a tall tree, out of reach.

"Half way down the slope we passed a village charmingly situated among trees and flowers, on the borders of a torrent which was dammed to feed some rice-mills. The natives were busy, in and around their houses; and a woman on seeing us, hastened to summon her children from the pool where they were drew nearer in coming from Kanasawa, the chapels and commemorative stones on the sacred hills, increased in number. After crossing a river on a fine wooden bridge, we found ourselves in the principal avenue, leading directly to the great square in front of the terraces, stairways and buildings of the temple. Around the first court are the houses of the bonzes, thrust behind each other like the side-scenes of a theatre, among trees planted around the wall of enclosure ; while two great ponds, of oval shape, occupy the centre of the square. These latter are connected by a broad canal, which is crossed by parallel bridges, each remarkable in its appearance. The one on the right is built of hewn stones of whitish granite, and is so nearly a perfect semicircle in its form, that one involuntarily wonders what gymnastic exercises were intended to be performed on it; but I take it to be the bridge of honor reserved for the gods and other good spirits, when they visit the temple. The bridge on the left is level, constructed of wood, covered with red lacquer, and with old copper ornaments on the railings. One pond is filled with the magnificent blossoms of the white lotus ; the other is splendid with the red lotus. Gold and crimson fish, and others with pearly fins swim in the crystal water between the leaves and flowers, and the black tortoise basks on the leaves.

"We now reach the second court, elevated above the first, and only to be entered by passing through the lodge appropriated to the divine guardians of the sanctuary. This building, facing the bridges, shelters under its high, peaked roof, two monstrous idols, one on each side. They are sculptured of wood, and

JAPANESE PILGRIMS.

coated with vermilion lacquer from head to foot. Their grimacing faces and enormous bodies are spotted with innumerable balls of chewed paper, which the native visitors throw at them in passing, with no more scruple than a band of mischievous school-boys. Nevertheless, this is a very serious act on the part of the pilgrims, for it assures them that the prayer written on the piece of paper which they chew, will probably reach its destination. In order to be entirely certain, they are required to purchase and suspend to the grating around the statues a pair of straw sandals large enough for the feet of the latter. Thousands of such sandals are constantly offered, and are allowed to hang on the grating until they drop to pieces from rottenness.

"A high terrace, surmounted by a grand staircase, towers over the second court. It is supported by a wall of cyclopean construction, and supports the principal temple, with the habitations of the chief bonzes The ornamentation of these buildings lacks neither taste nor proportion. It is chiefly applied to the portals, and to the brackets and cornices on which the roofs rest. The beautiful brown tint of the timber, which is almost the only material employed, is relieved by carvings, painted red or a brilliant green. To complete the effect of the picture, one must add its frame of immemorial trees and the incomparable brilliancy of the sky.

"The general view of the entire temple from the terrace almost inspired us with regret for the lost times, when the whole people were wont to unite, with their magistrates and ministers of worship, in a common act of religious adoration and patriotic enthusiasm. Even as the tribes of Israel in dedicating the Temple, the tribes of Nipor. and the neighboring isles formerly filled all these courts and avenues, under the eyes of the chiefs of the nation, grouped on the esplanade of the sanctuary. The view thence reaches to the sea, over the roofs and bridges, and the three portals dividing the grand avenue. With such a crowd surrounding these edifices, these pillars, these natural columns formed by the trunks of the cypresses, all the space, from the high terrace to the sea, would constitute but a single immense temple, sparkling with color and light, under the dome of the sky.

"Nothing could offer a ruder contrast to the sublime character of this picture, than the avenue to which we were conducted, in leaving the avenue of Hatchiman. It has been built, it is true, in an admirable situation, on the summit of a promontory which commands a view of the whole bay of Kamakura; but it is all the more saddening to find, amid such lovely scenery, a pretended sanctuary which only produces an impression of disgust. The principal building seemed at first to offer nothing remarkable ; there are only some insignificant gilded idols on the chief altar. In a lateral chapel one sees the god of wealth, armed with a miner's hammer. The bonzes, however, conducted us behind the altar, and there, in an obscure cage, like a prison, and as high as a tower, they lighted two lanterns and hoisted them slowly up a kind of mast. Then by the wavering light, almost lost in the shadows of the roof, we found ourselves face to face with an enormous idol of gilded wood, thirty-five feet in height, holding in the right hand a sceptre, in the left a lotus, and wearing a triple tiara, composed of the heads of inferior deities. This is one of the means by which the bonzes excite the superstitious imagination of the people, and keep them in a state of perpetual imbecility.

"The monument dedicated to Daïboodhs, that is, the Great Boodha, may be considered as the most complete work of the Japanese genius, in regard both to art and to the religious sentiment. The temple of Hatchiman has already given us an example of the profit which native art has learned to draw from nature, in easily producing that impression of religious majesty, which we associate, at home, with Gothic architecture. The temple of Daïboodhs [known to the English and American residents in Japan by the name of *Dyboots*] has, in many respects, a very different character. In place of grand and broad dimensions, of that unbounded space which sinks from gateway to gateway to the sea, a solitary, mysterious retreat was sought, such as might dispose the spirit to expect some supernatural revelation. The road, avoiding all habitations, directs itself towards the mountains; it winds, at first, between hedges of tall shrubs; then we see nothing before us but a straight path, ascending through foliage and flowers: then it turns, as if seeking some remote goals and all at once appears at the bottom of the alley, a gigantic seated divinity of bronze, with folded hands, and head gently inclined in an attitude of contemplative ecstasy.

"The involuntary shock which one feels, on the first appearance of this grand figure, soon gives place to admiration. There is an irresistible charm in the posture of Daïboodhs, in the harmony of his bodily proportions, in the noble simplicity of his drapery, and in the calmness and serenity of his countenance. A dense belt of foliage, over which tower a few beautiful groups of trees, is the only inclosure of the sacred place, the silence and solitude of which is undisturbed. We hardly distinguish the modest hermitage of the officiating priest, concealed in the foliage. The altar, where a little incense burns at the foot of the divinity, consists of a table of bronze, with two lotus vases of the same metal, and of admirable workmanship. The azure of the sky, the grand gloom of the statue, the austere tint of the bronze, the brilliancy of the flowers, and the varied verdure of the hedges and thickets, fill this retreat with the richest effects of light and colors.

"The figure of Daïboodhs, with the base upon which it rests, is a little more than sixty-five feet high. It does not equal in elevation the statue of San Carlo Borromeo, near Arona, on Lake Maggiore; but the latter leaves the spectator as cold as if it were merely a trigonometric signal. The interiors of both colossal statues have been utilized, more or less skillfully. The European tourists seat themselves in the nose of the cardinal; the Japanese descend by a staircase into the foundation of their Daïboodhs, where they find a quiet oratory, the altar of which receives a ray of the sun through an opening in the folds of the god's bronze mantle."

In a chapter on the bonzes, who officiate in these temples, M. Humbert gives the following views in regard to the modification which the original Buddhist religion has undergone in Japan : —

"Buddhism is a flexible, conciliating, insinuating faith, accommodating itself to the genius and the usages of the most diverse races. From their very first entrance into Japan, the bonzes succeeded in obtaining the charge of the ancient relics and even of the chapels of the saints, and preserving them within the bounds of their own sanctuaries. They speedily added to their ceremonies symbols borrowed from the ancient national worship ; and finally, in order more thoroughly to confound the two religions, they introduced into their temples both Japanese saints clothed with the titles and attributes of Hindoo divinities, and the Hindoo divinities transformed into Japanese saints. Owing to this combination, which is known under the name of Rioobou-Sintoo, Buddhism became the dominant religion of Japan.

"At first it was the great Boodh of India, to whom colossal statues — of which the Daïboodhs of Kamakura furnishes the best type — were erected. Afterwards the Japanese idea of a supreme divinity was personified in the fantastic image of Amida, who is represented under nine different forms, symbolizing his incarnation and his essential perfections, — one of the latter being expressed in the emblem of a dog's head. Among the auxiliary gods who serve as mediators between men and the supreme Being, the favor of the Japanese people is principally bestowed upon Quannon, who possesses the most frequented temple in Yedo, and in Miako the famous temple of the Thirty-three Thousand Three Hundred and Thirty-three Genii (pronounced in Japanese, *Sanman sansin sanbiak sansin santaï*). This divinity rests on a lotus-flower, the left leg doubled under the body; the head is covered with a veil which falls on the shoulders. The idol has no less than forty-six arms, bearing all sorts of attributes which attest his power."

CHAPTER IX.

THE HIGHWAY TO YEDO.

THE Tokaïdo, or great highway of Japan, passes near Yokohama, and strikes the coast at Kanagawa, on the opposite side of the harbor. When the traveller takes the land route to Yedo, he is obliged to accept the escort of a troop of mounted *yakounins*. M. Humbert, on setting out for the capital, ordered the latter to await him at the river Lokgo, which is the official limit fixed for the excursions of the foreign residents of Yokohama in that direction. "We crossed to Kanagawa," he says, "where our horses awaited us, and enjoyed one more hour of liberty in following at our ease the Tokaïdo. The highway was filled with two interminable files of travellers, on foot, on horseback, in palanquins and cangos; those going to the capital taking like us the right side of the road, and those returning from it taking the left.

"A halt was made at the tea-house of Mancïa, all open, both the main building and the wings, to a crowd of comers and goers. The matting was entirely hidden by the groups of picturesque feasters; the rear wall was taken up with furnaces, steaming boilers, shelves of utensils, and provisions; rapid waiters circulated on all sides, distributing with grace the lacquered plates laden with tea, cups of saki, fried fish, cakes, and the fruits of the season. Before the door, seated on the broad and short benches of the inn, mechanics and coolies refreshed themselves with fans, and women lighted their pipes at the common brazier. All at once a movement of horror takes place among the guests and the waiters; a detachment of police officers, escorting a criminal, arrive to take refreshments. With all haste the two-sworded gentlemen are supplied with boiling tea or tepid saki, while the coolies who carry the prisoner in a basket of woven bamboo without any apparent opening, deposit their burden on the ground, and with a long piece of crape begin to dry the sweat which trickles down their shoulder-blades. As to the prisoner, who may be espied doubled up within, with haggard eye, and unkempt beard and hair, he will be shut up and tortured in the prisons of Yedo, to answer for the crimes of which he is accused in a placard suspended from the basket.

"At about twelve miles from Kanagawa, the pleasant suburb of Kawasaki extends along the right bank of the Lokgo to the long bars formed by the deposits of this muddy stream. They may be distinguished in the bay for a long distance, as a line of demarkation between the anchorage of Kanagawa and that of Yedo. Kawasaki has several temples, among which that of Daïsi-Gwanara seems to me to be one of the purest specimens of Buddhist architecture in Japan. I have heard different accounts of the worship to which it is consecrated; among others a marvelous legend concerning the saint who is the special object of veneration. He attained the virtue of contemplation to such a degree that he did not perceive that a charcoal

A STREET SCENE IN JAPAN.

fire, in a pan before him, had destroyed his hands while he was abstracted in his devotions.

"The passage of the Lokgo was effected in the large flat boats which are freighted, pell-mell, with travellers and horses. Our yakounins awaited us on the opposite shore. After the usual indispensable compliments, each one mounted his horse, and we set out at a rapid trot, in a complete confusion, which, nevertheless, gradually gave way to a regular order of march.

"Although the Tokaïdo, in general, does not fall below any of the great roads of Europe, and has the advantage throughout its whole extent, of being bordered with sidewalks shaded by avenues of splendid trees, it is most neglected in the neighborhood of Yedo. A day of rain converts into pools of mud the streets of the numerous villages which are traversed after leaving Kanagawa. In this respect as in many others, the Japanese manifest at the same time a very remarkable intelligence in the works of civilization, and, when they come to apply it, a careless disregard of details none the less remarkable.

"At last we reach the limits of the municipality of Yedo. A short halt at the door of one of the numerous tea-houses of the village of Omori introduces us to a gay society of good citizens of the capital, accompanied by their wives and children. Except the costume, it is a repetition of one of our own suburban scenes. Other groups, not less noisy, besiege a great store-house of articles made of rushes, straw, and bamboo, which is announced afar off by a confused symphony of flageolets, trumpets, and Pan's-pipes, given to childish amateurs for trial. An infinite variety of children's toys, fancy hats, animals made of plaited straw, painted and varnished, are displayed. We see among them the bear of Yeso, the monkey of Niphon, the domesticated buffalo, and the centenary turtle, trailing after him the tufts of marine herbs which grow upon his shell.

" But time presses, and the sight of the anchorage, covered with white sails, excites our impatience. Soon we skirt the shore of the bay. The highway rests on strong foundations of sunken stones; but the waves which formerly broke upon them, now die among the reeds and sea-weed. On our left extends a grove of pine and cypress, above which flocks of ravens are wheeling, and our guides point out to us a distant clearing as the place for capital executions, at least for the southern part of the city, there being a second for the northern part. Nothing can equal the gloomy aspect of these places. Even if one is fortunate enough to avoid seeing the exposed heads or the bodies abandoned to dogs and birds, one cannot perceive without horror the recent earth which covers the remains of the victims; the pillar of granite with some unknown dismal inscription; the plank shed which serves as a shelter for the officers who are present at the execution; and, towering over all, the gigantic statue of Boodha, sad symbol of implacable expiation and unconsoled death.

" After passing this spot, we enter that suburb of Yedo which has the worst fame, — Sinagawa, which commences two miles to the southward of the city proper, with which it unites at the gate of the Takanawa quarter. The Japanese government has adopted the strict rule that foreigners who come to Yedo, or who reside in that city, shall not pass through Sinagawa except by daylight and under a strong escort. It is not because the permanent population of the suburb is not entirely inoffensive; for it is chiefly composed of boatmen, fishers, and laborers. But these latter inhabit the cabins along the strand, while both sides of the Tokaïdo are bordered, without interruption, with the very worst kind of tea-houses. You find there the same scum of society as in the great cities of Europe and America, and besides, a very dangerous class of men, vagabonds, peculiar to the capital of Japan. These are the *lonins*, unemployed officers belonging to the caste of the Samouraïs, who have therefore the privilege of carrying two sabres. Some are the sons of good families, who have been turned out of their homes by their dissipated lives; others have lost by bad conduct their former places in the service of the Tycoon or in the military household of some daimio; and others, again, have been discharged by some chief who has been forced to reduce his expenses by diminishing the number of his suite.

"The *lonin*, deprived of the pay upon which he lives, and knowing nothing beyond the trade of arms, has generally no other resource, while awaiting a new service, than to betake himself to the retreats of vice, and perform some ignoble office or other, in return for the hospitality. The custom which he attracts adds new elements of danger to those with which the suburb abounds. He establishes an organization, even a sort of discipline, in the midst of disorder and crime. There are chiefs of *lonins* whom bands of miserable wretches follow with a blind obedience. To such the mysterious agents who offer themselves to be the instruments of vengeance for family or political hate, among the Japanese nobility, address themselves in carrying out their bloody plans. Like certain streets in the neighborhood of the Tower of London, the suburb of Sinagawa is abandoned by the police during the greater part of the night. Even the women sally out upon the Tokaïdo, and assail the belated travellers, in order to force them into the houses where they serve. The *lonins* are so entirely conscious of the abject condition in which they live, that when they issue from their lairs, they usually take the precaution of concealing the face under a large hat with depressed brim, or by means of a piece of crape in which they envelop the head, so that nothing but the eyes can be seen. In the immediate neighborhood of this class, on the higher parts of the Takanawa quarter, the Japanese government has established the foreign legations."

ENTRANCE TO THE AMERICAN LEGATION, YEDO

CHAPTER X.

LIFE IN YEDO.

"ACCORDING to a Japanese proverb," says M. Humbert, "one must live in Yedo, in order to be happy.

"If this be true, happiness is not easily attained by Europeans living in Japan. At the time of my visit, only the diplomatic agents enjoyed the right of residing in the capital of the Tycoon; and two or three years' experience of the conditions attached to the exercise of this privilege had led all of them to decide to transfer their real domiciles to Yokohama. They gave the impression of having been treated at Yedo very much like prisoners of distinction, free to go and come within a certain radius, and watched by day and by night with the most unwearied solicitude. Nevertheless, in spite of the annoyances of this repellant policy of the Japanese authorities, it must be remarked in its favor, that its effect was to excite the spirit of investigation to the highest point, by adding the attraction of mystery, the spur of difficulties to be overcome, to the interest of the field of study.

"We owe to M. Lindau an excellent general estimate of the extent, the population, and the topography of the city of Yedo. According to his calculation this capital, so remarkable in all respects, covers a space of eighty-five square *kilometres* (about twenty-three square miles, English), and contains about one million eight hundred thousand inhabitants. He adds that in 1858, the elements of this enormous population were thus divided: the respectable middle-class, merchants, and artisans, 572,848; the daimios, their retainers and followers, very nearly 500,000; the house and court of the Tycoon, estimated at 180,000; the members of the priesthood at probably 200,000; travellers and pilgrims, also 200,000; beggars and parias, 50,000. I have reason to believe that, in spite of the fluctuations to which the population of Yedo is subjected, more than that of any other city, the calculations of M. Lindau may be adopted at present (1868), as being as nearly as possible correct.

" The southern part of the city, in which the foreign legations are established, contains eight wards, occupying all the space comprised between the suburb of Sinagawa on the south, the bay on the east, the outer moat of the Tycoon's castle on the north, and the fields of the province of Mousasi, on the west. All these southern quarters of Yedo are essentially plebeian. They even contain a large agricultural population, occupied with the cultivation of kitchen-gardens, rice-fields, and all the arable lands which the habitations have not yet covered. The latter are a multitude of miserable dwellings, tenanted by fishers, laborers, mechanics, retail merchants, officers of the lowest rank, and the proprietors of the commonest eating-houses.

" A few seignorial residences interrupt the uniformity of the wooden buildings by the monotonous lines of their long, whitewashed walls. The temples and dwellings of the bonzes are scattered everywhere, except in the two bay-quarters; Takanawa, alone, has more than thirty of them. But the devotional spirit must have emigrated to the northern part of the city; for the government has conveniently selected all the buildings necessary for the reception of embassies and the residence of foreign legations, from among the temples of the southern quarter.

"Since 1858, the embassies which the Tycoon has received have generally reached his capital by sea. One must not suppose, however, that such an event is marked by discharges of artillery, or any other imposing features; if the foreign representatives desired the like, it is doubtful whether they could succeed. They are forced to pass from one deception to another.

"In the first place, the voyage from Yokohama to Yedo suffices to banish all preconceived ideas of the approach to a sea-port which has nearly two millions of inhabitants. The distance is about fifteen nautical miles. One would expect to pass through an uninterrupted fleet of junks going to, or coming from, the great city, on its only maritime highway; but there is no such fleet. After leaving the anchorage at Kanagawa, the bay is almost deserted, and even the fishing-boats do not appear until after passing the sand-bars of Kawasaki. In Japan, there is almost a complete absence of commerce by sea. A few junks are engaged in the coasting trade in the bay of Yedo, but they scarcely pass the limits of the first line of customs: they stop at Usaga, whence their cargoes are sent to the capital on pack-horses. The Tokaido and other high roads of secondary importance, are the main arteries which supply Yedo, and they appear all the more animated from their contrast with the abandoned watery ways.

"No unwalled city presents a more inhospitable appearance than Yedo, when seen from the bay. It resembles an immense park, the entrance to which is prohibited. The richly wooded hills are dotted with *chalets* and old temples with enormous roofs; at their feet extend long streets of wooden houses and some buildings with white walls; but along the whole great extent of the arc of shore, from Sinagawa to the landing-place, nothing can be distinguished which answers to our notions of quays, port, or embarkation. Everywhere there are walls, boarded inclosures, palisades; no jetties, steps, or anything whatever which seems to invite a landing. Even the place of entrance to the city is concealed behind a palisade of large piles, and consists only of a few old planks laid on supports, and connecting with a terrace in front of the custom-house.

"Here the officials of the Japanese government welcome the representatives of foreign nations, and beg them to accept the services of the guard of honor which the Tycoon has appointed for their protection. These formalities over, the principal personages of the two nations mount their horses or palanquins, and the procession, properly organized, issues from its prison by the gate opening on the Tokaido. After marching for fifteen or twenty minutes between two crowds of the curious of both sexes, gathered from the shops, the tea-houses, and the baths of the neighborhood, in a *negligé*, which is doubtless very picturesque but

AMERICAN LEGATION, YEDO.

which does not add to the dignity of the spectacle, the hills of Takanawa are ascended, the procession enters the solitary alleys of this cloistered region, and soon reaches the threshold of the other privileged prison which bears the name of ' Legation.'

"The structures of the temples of Tjoodji, seat of the Dutch Legation, had been put at my disposal by the representative of Holland, in Japan. As they were then unoccupied, they served as a residence to the members of the Swiss Legation, not only for excursions to the capital, but also for a prolonged sojourn there. If the peace of His Tycoonal Majesty's Government had not been so gravely troubled thereby, I should have willingly passed several of the summer months in the Tjoodji. The little deserted temple is surrounded, on all sides, with other sacred places which are almost equally solitary, and there the quiet of the country may be enjoyed, in proximity to the animation of the great streets of the city.

"The principal façade of the formerly sacred buildings is half concealed behind clumps of evergreen trees. On approaching the portico, I found it occupied by a group of Japanese officers. One of them saluted me in Dutch, announcing that he had been charged by his government to offer me his services as interpreter; he then presented to me the captain of the guard, who, he informed me, was one of the aids-de-camp of the Tycoon. The latter had established himself in one of the ancient sanctuaries opening on the portico, and declared that he should pass his nights there.

"At one of the extremities of the mass of buildings, we established the kitchen and a little studio for the use of the skillful photographer Beato, who had recently arrived in Yokohama from India and China ; and we reserved a long gallery for the exposition of such objects of art and industry as might be brought to us for examination. The other extremity, which formed a semicircular inclosure in the rear of the temple, contained three adjoining rooms : the *salon*, my bedroom, and the dining-room, all three surrounded by an open gallery. This was the quietest and most agreeable portion of the *bonzerie*. A pond, bordered with iris and water-lilies, occupied the centre of the inclosure ; it was fed by a spring which issued from a neighboring grotto, draped with climbing plants. Beside this grotto, in a niche, surrounded with foliage, there was an ancient idol of sandstone, with its own little altar still remaining. A rustic bridge across the brook led to a path which wound among the trees and the rocks up to the highest palisades of the inclosure. There, under a shelter of pines and laurels, was a rock-hewn place of rest, whence the eye overlooked the gardens and buildings of the Tjoodji, and the forts and anchorage in the distance.

"At the hour of sunset, this little picture was full of beauty. The sky and the bay were enlivened by the richest colors ; the foliage of the hills gleamed in a sudden illumination, and the pond below was tinted with purple. Then the shadows invaded the verdant inclosure and by degrees mounted to the summits of the trees which surrounded it. The birds from the strand came in great numbers to roost there. Soon the tufted tops of the foliage were darkly cut against the silvery sky, and the pond reflected, like a mirror, the trembling rays of the stars.

" Then the night-guard began to visit, in silence, all the hidden nooks and corners of the place. A sentinel, furnished with a lantern of colored paper, was posted at intervals. The Japanese guards squatted down quietly, with these lanterns at their feet. One was at the angle of the portico of the *salon;* another at the resting-place on the height; a third, near the bridge over the brook; others, again, behind the temple, at the door of my bedroom, and near the dining-room. The patrols were promptly made. When they approached, the sentinels rose and cried ' *Dalé-da?* ' The reply was the pass-word for the night. The captain of the guard gave it to me regularly in writing, in Japanese and Dutch.

" The spectacle of this military array followed me even to my bed. Across the paper screens of my rooms I could see the lanterns of the sentinels shining in the garden and on the portico; and that, which ought to have given me the highest sense of security, was, that no obstacle intervened between my guards and myself, for all our doors were movable and quite free of locks. With the exception of the Toodji, I cannot speak, from experience, of the interiors of the foreign legations. At the time of my visit they were closed, the members of the diplomatic corps having retired to Yokohama. I have reason to believe that, with some slight variations, they offer to their hosts conditions of life very analogous to those which I have here outlined.

" The most ancient of the foreign residences at Yedo is that of Akabané, situated in the quarter of that name. The Japanese government designed it, in 1858, for a caravanserai of all ambassadors. They were there furnished with quarters, without furniture, or any other comforts than matting and the native screens. One after the other, M. Donker-Curtius (Holland), Admiral Poutiatine (Russia), Baron Gros (France), and Count Eulenburg (Prussia), lodged there. Since 1861, however, the Akabané has not been occupied. The American Legation occupies the sanctuary of Djemfkousi, in the vicinity. When I visited it, there remained only the temple, the belfry, and some outhouses. All the rest of the structures had been leveled to the earth by a fire, accompanied with works of demolition and salvage, the efficacy of which I could appreciate from the circumstance that the books saved from the flames had been thrown into the tank for preservation!

"The Tosendji, the seat of the British Legation, is the most beautiful and spacious of all the foreign residences. This ancient sanctuary, the property of Prince Shendai, was put at the disposition of Lord Elgin, by the government of the Tycoon, in 1858. It is more than half a mile to the southward of the Tjoodji, and is bordered by hills, adorned with avenues and groves, where the bamboo, the palm, the azalea, the weeping willow, and the chestnut, are grouped with pines from fifty to one hundred feet in height. But there is scarcely a nook of this charming residence which does not recall some gloomy memory. The foot of the flag-staff has been dyed by the blood of the Japanese interpreter Denkoushki; the steps of the portico, the court-yard, the temple, the first story of the legation, became, in the nocturnal attack of July 8, 1861, the scene of a frightful struggle, which left five dead and eighteen wounded on the field; and finally, on the verandah, toward the garden, a year later, two English marines fell, after having mortally wounded one of their assassins.

"The diplomatic agents of the powers which have concluded treaties with Japan have not remained inactive, one may well believe, in view of the situation thus created for them in Yedo. After maturely deliberating upon the course which they should take, they exacted and obtained from the Tycoon the concession of a locality where it would be possible to unite the forces of all the legations, to put them in a state of defense, and secure their communications with the vessels of war at the anchorage.

"There was then, at the southern extremity of the quarter of Takanawa, a very spacious public garden called Goten-yama, on a cluster of hills commanding the Tokaido, the anchorage and the battery of Odaïwa. It was agreed that this place offered all the desirable advantages, and, without further delay, the axe was laid to the orchards of blossoming peach trees and the groves of cedars, where the citizens of Yedo were wont to come with their families, to contemplate the view of the bay, to take their tea, drink their *saki*, and enjoy the musical or saltatory performances of the beauties of the neighborhood. When all had been well destroyed, graded, leveled; when the new Britannic Legation displaying its imposing façade, its elegant galleries, and its immense roofs, had given to the nobles and peasants of Yedo a foretaste of the magnificence which the future quarter of the Ministers of the West promised to their city, all at once, on a fine winter night, the anchorage was made splendid by an immense bonfire kindled on the Goten-yama. As soon as it had been completed, the first European palace erected in the capital of the Tycoon burned from top to bottom. The others remain, either as foundations only or as plans on paper, and the representatives of the powers friendly to Japan still reside at Yokohama" [in 1868].

NOON SCENE ON A JAPANESE CANAL

CHAPTER XI.

WALKS IN YEDO.

"THROUGH the southern suburbs, which stretched toward the country, to the southwest of our residence, we discovered but one respectable and well kept road, — that which led to the principal temple of Megouro. Nearly all the Europeans who have lived in Yedo know Mengourou, as this antique sanctuary and the graceful tea-houses around it are vulgarly called. A little beyond, a hill cut into the shape of Fusi-yama attracts, at certain seasons of the year, especially at the time when the orchards blossom, a crowd of native promenaders, belonging to the lower classes of Yedo society.

"The dwellings of the *petite noblesse*, that is, the subalterns in the Tycoon's service, are scattered in great numbers through the district, and there are also two race-courses for the exercises of the officers in horsemanship. In this neighborhood, however, we found neither palaces nor large temples. Two other adjoining quarters exhibited a few rustic dwellings of the bonzes, and some ancient monuments shaded by great cedar trees; but we were impatient to discover the most interesting parts of the city, and finally determined to examine the northern districts. After having carefully traced out a route on the excellent Japan ese map of Yedo, we announced to our yakounins, one fine day, that we were going to make an excursion on foot in the direction of the Castle.

"This information did not especially please them; for greatly as they delight in escorting their foreign hosts on horseback, and in trotting with them rapidly through the long streets of the capital, it is equally disagreeable to them to take part in pedestrian excursions during which their vigilance is constantly racked by the curiosity of the Occidentals.

"Two of the officials of the Legation, who had gained the good graces of the principal officers of the guard, hit upon the idea of furnishing them with a subject of distraction, for the route. They persuaded them to profit by the occasion, and learn to keep step in walking. All the yakounins, one after the other, set themselves to work, to follow conscientiously the recommendation and example of their instructors. The citizens of Yedo stopped to observe the unusual movement, and even the officers could not refrain from occasionally looking down and watching their feet. Sometimes, even, delicately lifting their broad silk petticoat-pantaloons, they presented a superb array of naked calves, blue cotton socks, and straw sandals.

"As our march was further prolonged, their headdresses, also, suffered an ingenious modification. The yakounins took off their heavy lacquered hats, and suspended them at their girdles like bucklers; after which, seizing a fan, which they always carry behind the neck, under the collar of their jacket, they converted it into a visor by thrusting the end under the knob of hair which surmounts their shaven foreheads. The tableau would not be complete, if I did not add that we ourselves, in regard to costume, were very nearly in harmony with our surroundings. Yedo is perhaps the only city of the world where the European succeeds in liberating himself from the despotism of fashion. It is impossible to resist the example of such an immense population, which, except at court and during solemn festivals, knows no other rule in relation to garments, but that of dressing as one pleases and undressing at will, leaving to one's neighbor the fullest liberty of doing the same thing.

"Thus the appearance of our party, which would have occasioned a mob in any densely populated part of Europe, did not cause the least sensation in the capital of the Tycoon. People looked at us, of course, with a very legitimate curiosity; but fingers were only occasionally pointed at our cigars or at the revolvers in our belts.

"From morning until night, the low streets and quays of Takanawa are crowded with people. The stable population of the quarter seemed to me to have no other industry except to raise, in one manner or another, a light tribute from those arriving and departing. Here, tobacco is cut and sold; there, rice is hulled and made into biscuits; everywhere saki is sold, tea, dried fish, water-melons, an infinite variety of cheap fruits and other comestibles, spread on tables in the open air, or under sheds and on the shelves of innumerable restaurants. In all directions, coolies, boatmen, and bearers of cargoes offer their services. In some lateral streets, stalls may be hired for pack-horses, and stables for the buffaloes which bring to market the products of the surrounding country. They are harnessed to small rustic carts, the only wheeled vehicles which one meets in Yedo.

"The singers, the dancers, the wandering jugglers who come to try their success in the capital, make their first appearance at the doors of the tea-houses of Takanawa. Among the singers there are those who form a privileged class, but subjected to a certain supervision by the police. They may be known by their large flat hats, thrown back from the temples; they always go in pairs, or in fours when two dancers accompany the two singers.

"The favorite jugglers at the Japanese street-corners are young boys, who, before commencing their tricks, conceal their heads in large hoods, surmounted by a tuft of cock's feathers and a small scarlet mask representing the muzzle of a dog. These poor children, in bending and curving themselves, one upon the other, to the monotonous sound of the tambourine of their conductor, present the appearance of a really grotesque and fantastic struggle between two animals, with monstrous heads and human limbs.

"In the deafening sounds of all these diversions in the spaces filled by the public, there was frequently mixed the noise of the cymbals and bells of the mendicant brotherhood. I saw, for the first time, some whose heads were not tonsured, and inquired what the order was to which they belonged. Our interpreter answered that they were laymen, simple citizens of Yedo, making a business of devotion. Although they were all similarly clad in white, in token of mourning or penitence, those who carried a bell, a long stick,

LITTLE JUGGLERS IN THE STREETS OF YEDO

some books in a basket, and wore a large white hat with a picture of Fusi-yama on the side, were returning from a pilgrimage to the holy mountain, made by public charity; while the others, with a cymbal at the girdle, an immense black and yellow hat, and a heavy box on the back, were probably small ruined merchants, who had become colporteurs and exhibitors of idols, in the pay of some monastery.

"On the heights above the landing-place, a long street leaves the Tokaïdo, cuts obliquely through the chain of hills where the legations are situated, and traverses in a straight line, from south to north, the northern part of Takanawa. We followed this street to the end, and passed, successively, through three very distinct zones of the social life of Yedo. The first, with its motley crowd of people living in the open air, I have already described.

"Behind our monastic hills we found a population entirely sedentary, occupied, within their dwellings, in various manual labors. The work-shops were announced, at a distance, by significant signs,—sometimes a board cut in the form of a sandal, sometimes, an enormous umbrella of waxed paper, spread open like an awning, over the shop; or a quantity of straw hats of all sizes, dangling from the peak of the roof down to the door. We see, in passing, the armorers and polishers, busy in mounting coats of mail, iron war-fans, and sabres. An old artisan, naked, crouched on a mat, pulls the bellows of the forge with his left heel, and at the same time hammers with his right hand the iron bar which his left hand holds on the anvil. His son, also naked, takes the iron bars with the tongs and passes them to his father, as they become red-hot.

"Little by little the road which we are following becomes deserted. We enter the vast solitude of a collection of seignorial residences. On our right extend the magnificent shades of the park of the Prince of Satsouma; on our left the wall of inclosure of a palace of the Prince of Arima. When we had turned the northwestern angle of this wall, we found ourselves before the principal front of the building, opposite to which there was a plantation of trees, bathed by the waters of a limpid river which separates the quarter of Takanawa from that of Atakosta.

"Mr. Beato set to work to procure a photograph of this peaceful picture, when two officers of the prince hastily approached him, and insisted that he should desist from the operation. M. Metman begged them to go first and ascertain the commands of their master. The officers went to deliver the message; returning in a few minutes, they declared that the prince absolutely refused to permit that any view whatever of his palace should be taken. Beato bowed respectfully, and ordered the porters to carry away the instrument. The officers withdrew, satisfied, without suspecting that the artist had had time to take two negatives during their brief absence.

"The yakounins of our escort, impassive witnesses of the scene, were unanimous in applauding the success of the stratagem. But when the artist announced his intention of also taking, in the neighborhood, a photograph of the cemetery of the Tycoons, it became their turn to oppose a resistance to the plan, which no

JAPANESE BLACKSMITHS.

arguments could bend. We were even obliged to give up the idea of entering the sepulchral grounds, although we could very distinctly see the high red pagoda and the sombre clumps of cypress.

We crossed a river by an arched bridge, not far from the place where the American secretary, Heusken, was murdered; and, leaving on our right some houses which a recent great conflagration had spared, we passed an open space, with a field for archery on one side, and on the other the walls behind which rise the groves and temple-roofs of Soïosti, the great monastery which has the honor of receiving the Tycoons in their last earthly dwelling. They rest there under the combined protection of the two religions of the empire. Buddhism, it is true, enjoys a supremacy in this place, and possesses more than seventy sacred edifices; but the ancient gods, Hatchiman, Benten, Inari, have each their chapels, and there is a grand temple dedicated to the worship of the Kamis.

"In this direction is the Tycoon's place of embarkation, in the island of Amagoten, which forms a regular parallelogram, and is reached by two bridges, prohibited to the public. I have made the circuit of the island in the consular boat: the walls of inclosure, the steps, the pavilions of the landing-place, the overshadowing masses of verdure, are admirable in their grand simplicity. The great trees which line both sides of the river shelter its deep, pure waters under their dense roofs of foliage. The ministers of France, Holland, England, and America, made a combined effort to obtain from the Japanese government the cession of the island, for the purpose of establishing their legations there; but they did not succeed, because the execution of the plan would have exacted the use of the whole island, while the government was only willing to abandon a very small part of it.

" We continued our journey northwards. On the left fourteen small adjacent temples, those of Saisoostji, extend along the foot of the hills of Atagosa-yama, separated by a large brook from the highway. Each of these temples has its special bridge, its gateway, its little level of turf, inclosed by chapels and the dwellings of the bonzes; while, in the rear, may be distinguished the chapel of ablutions, the sacred grove, and the roofs of the sanctuary. The sixth, however, is an exception to the others. When we have crossed the threshold, we see before us a great paved court-yard, in the midst of which stands a majestic altar of granite. Then, after passing through the sacred gate, we find ourselves face to face with two candelabra placed at the foot of an esplanade, reached by a staircase; then there is a second, bordered by huge trees, the branches of which interlace like the arches of a Gothic cathedral. Through the foliage we distinguish a broad stone stairway, the summit of which is lost to sight behind the masses of verdure.

" We gradually mount to the summit of the hill: there are about a hundred steps. On the right hand, a path of easier ascent runs obliquely along the wooded slopes, by means of terraces which are provided with resting-places. A ruined oratory, with two insignificant idols, one standing on a lotus, the other seated on a tortoise, and long covered galleries, radiating around a tea-house, occupy the summit of Atagosa-yama.

The young waitresses attached to the place hasten to serve us with refreshments, and we take a moment's rest before visiting the pavilions, which at the two extremities of the terrace rise freely against the sky.

"At last the moment comes when the whole city is revealed to the view. We will begin with the southern pavilion: at first the eyes are dazzled with the extent and brilliancy of the picture. The sun sinks to the horizon, in a cloudless sky; the transparency of the atmosphere allows us to distinguish the forts on the luminous surface of the bay. But over all the space extending from the anchorage to the foot of the hill upon which we stand, the vision knows not where to linger: there is a veritable ocean of long streets, of white walls and gray roofs. Nothing interrupts the monotony of the panorama, except, here and there, the dark foliage of clumps of trees, or some temple, the gable of which towers like a wave over the undulating lines of the dwellings. In the nearer neighborhood, a broad cavity drawn across the streets, as if a hurricane had passed that way, marks the course of a recent conflagration, and, still further off, the sombre mass of the hills consecrated to the sepulchres of the Tycoons presents the appearance of a solitary island rising out of a raging sea.

"The panorama furnished by the northern pavilion is still more uniform, if possible. It embraces the quarters specially inhabited by the nobility, and the ramparts and leafy parks of the Imperial Castle bound the view, on the horizon. The *daïmio-yaskis*, or seignorial residences, to which we improperly give the name of palaces, only differ from each other in their extent and dimensions. The most opulent and the most modest present the same type of architecture, the same simple character. The external circuit consists of ranges of buildings reserved for the servants and men-at-arms of the prince: they are but a single story in height, and form a long square which is always surrounded by a ditch. A single roof covers them all, with no other break in it than the front of a portal, generally inserted in the centre of one of the sides of the parallelogram. There is not often any other exit through the outer wall than through this portal. The windows in the buildings are very numerous, low and broad, regularly set in two parallel rows, and usually closed with wooden gratings.

"In the interior, a number, more or less considerable, of low houses, divided into regular compartments, like the barracks of the yakounins at Benten, are arranged diagonally all around, or, at least, along the longer sides of the inclosing buildings. Here the seignorial troops encamp. An open space leads to the inner inclosure, which is the residence proper. The dependencies of the palace face the military quarter. The principal parts of the dwelling and the verandah open upon an interior court and the garden, which has always a pond surrounded with fresh foliage. Such is the silent inviolate asylum, where the haughty daimio withdraws in the bosom of his family during the six months of the year which the laws of the Empire oblige him to spend at the capital.

"We could only estimate the conditions under which the Japanese nobility reside in Yedo from what we caught in this bird's-eye view. No European has ever crossed the threshold of their residences. The ministers of the Tycoon have never admitted into their own dwellings any foreign ambassador.

"The panorama from Atagosa-yama only disclosed to us about one fourth part of the great capital. Towards the north, our view was obstructed by the walls surrounding the castle of the Tycoon. We therefore resolved to devote another day to the quarters in that direction, which form with the castle itself, the central part of Yedo. The walls appeared to us as two concentric circles, drawn by the blue lines of broad canals, communicating with each other and with the bay by means of numerous arms. We carried out the plan in a walk of four hours, during which there unfolded before our steps, like the windings of a mysterious labyrinth of stone, the ramparts, the towers, and the palaces within which the power of the Tycoons has found a shelter for more than two hundred years.

"It is an imposing spectacle, but it leaves a chilly impression on the mind. The political order of things instituted in Japan by the usurper Iyeyas vaguely recalls the régime of the Venetian Republic under the rule of the Council of Ten. If it has not the same grandeur, it possesses at least the same terrors, — the sombre majesty of the Chief of State, the impenetrable mystery of his government, the concealed and continuous action of a system of espionage officially arranged in all branches of the administration, and drawing after it, in the shadow, proscriptions, assassinations, secret executions.

"But we must not further extend the comparison with Venice. In Yedo one seeks in vain, over all the vast extent of the glacis of the castle, some monument which deserves to be mentioned beside the marvelous edifices of the Place of San Marco or the Riva de' Schiavoni. Artistic taste is completely wanting at the court of the Tycoons. It is left to the people, with poetry, religion, social life, with all superfluous things which only embarrass the movement of the political machine. From one end to the other of the administrative hierarchy, each official being flanked by a secretly appointed controller, the talents of the employés are exhausted in learning how to do nothing, and say nothing, which might furnish material for damaging reports. As to their private life, it is concealed, like that of the Japanese nobles, behind the walls of their domestic fortresses. While the streets inhabited by the common people, with all their dwellings open to the public view, are constantly animated with crowds of comers and goers of all ages and both sexes, in the aristocratic quarters one sees neither women nor children, unless in glimpses, through the grating of the windows, in the houses of the retainers.

"There are thus in Yedo two coexisting forms of society, one of which, armed and endowed with privileges, lives as if imprisoned in a vast citadel; and the other, disarmed, subject to the domination of the former, apparently enjoys all the advantages of liberty. But in reality a rod of iron is laid upon the people of Yedo. Out of five heads of families, one is always established by the government as an authority over the other four. The iniquitous laws punish a whole family, a district even, for the crime of one of the members. Neither the property nor the lives of the citizens are guarded by any legal protection. The extortions and the brutal acts of the two-sworded class remain for the most part unpunished. But the burgher turns for compensation to the charms which his good city offers him. If the rule of the Tycoons sometimes appears hard to him, he remembers that the Mikados have not always been good-natured, — that one of them, in ancient times, loved to display his skill as an archer in bringing down with his shafts the peasants whom he forced to climb trees as game.

"In countries fashioned by despotism, it is an embarrassing thing for the poor people to ascertain the proper limits of their patience. In a republic they become exacting, because the government opens to them the prospect of a continuous social amelioration, because every republican government falls short of the task imposed upon it by its own nature. But under the rule of individual will, on the contrary, the despot gets credit for not doing all the evil in his power. A Japanese emperor, who was born under the constellation of the Dog, ordered that all dogs should be respected as sacred animals, that they must not be killed, and must receive honorable sepulture when they died. A subject, whose dog had died, set to work to bury the body properly upon one of the sepulchral mounds. While on the way, and weary with the weight of the dead dog, he ventured to say to a neighbor that the Emperor's order seemed ridiculous to him. 'Beware how you complain,' the neighbor replied; 'our Emperor might just as well have been born under the sign of the Horse.'

"The first great line of defense of the castle is surrounded with water, except on the western side, where it communicates with the adjoining quarter of the city by the parade-ground belonging to the Tycoon. Ten arched wooden bridges are thrown across the broad moats: a strong detachment of the Tycoon's troops occupied the guard-house attached to the one which we crossed. The common soldiers are mountaineers of Akoni, who are allowed to return to their homes after a service of two or three years. Their uniform of blue cotton consists of close fitting pantaloons, and a shirt something like that of the Garibaldians. They wear cotton socks, and leathern sandals, and a large sabre with a lacquered scabbard is thrust through the girdle. The cartridge-box and bayonet are worn suspended on the right side. A pointed hat of lacquered paper completes their accoutrement, but they only put it on when mounting guard, or in going to drill.

"As to the muskets used in the Japanese army, although they all have percussion locks, they vary in calibre and construction. I saw four different kinds in the workshop of the barracks of Benten, where a yakounin introduced me. He showed me a Dutch model, then an arm of an inferior quality, from a workshop in Yedo, then an American musket, and finally a Minié rifle, the use of which a young officer was then teaching to a squad of soldiers in the court-yard. I noticed that the latter gave the words of command in Dutch. He held a ramrod in his right hand, and the grace of his movements, as well as the sweetness of his voice, made him resemble, at a little distance, a dancing-master directing the steps of his pupils with a fiddle-bow.

SOLDIER OF THE TYCOON.

" Notwithstanding their prompt intelligence of the great progress in the art of war realized by the Western nations, the Japanese have not yet been able to abolish the heavy military apparel of their feudal times. The helmet, the coat of mail, the halberd, the two-handed sword are still employed in their reviews and grand manœuvres. Bodies of archers still flank infantry columns equipped in the European manner, and chevaliers worthy of the times of the Crusades make their appearance in the dust of artillery trains.

" All the young officers are daily exercised, from an early age, in face-to-face combats, with the lance and two-handed sword, the rapier and the knife. The quarter which we traversed possessed two race-courses and several buildings destined for exercises in equitation and fencing. We saw the masters passing, accompanied by their pupils and followed by servants who bore lances and sabres of wood, as well as gloves, masks, and breast-plates, such as are used in the fencing-halls of the German universities. The jousters, still hot from their encounters, had thrown their silk mantles over one shoulder, and opened their close jackets upon the breast. Thus relieved, they walked along at their ease, silent and dignified, as is the manner of gentlemen.

" I was several times present at the fencing-matches of the yakounins. The champions salute each other before the attack : sometimes he who is on the defensive drops one knee upon the earth, in order the better to cross weapons and to parry with more force the blows of his adversary. Each pass is accompanied with theatrical poses and expressive gestures ; each blow provokes passionate exclamations from one or the other; then the judges intervene and emphatically pronounce their verdict, until finally a cup of tea appears as the interlude. There is even a variety of fencing for the Japanese ladies. Their arm is a lance with a curved blade, something like that of the Polish scythemen. They hold it with the point directed toward the earth, and wield it according to rule in a series of attitudes, poses, and cadenced movements, which would furnish charming subjects for a ballet. I was not allowed to see much of this graceful display, which I happened to get sight of in passing before a half-open court-yard. My yakounins closed the gate, assuring me that the customs of the country do not allow witnesses to see these feminine feats of arms.

"In their weapons the Japanese nobles exhibit the greatest luxury, and take the most pride. Especially their sabres, the temper of which is unrivaled, are generally enriched, at the hilt and on the scabbard, with metal ornaments, graven and cut with great skill. But the principal value of their arms consists in their antiquity and celebrity. Each sword in the old families of the daimios, has its history and traditions, the glory of which is measured by the blood which it has shed. A new sword must not long remain virgin in the hands of him who buys it; until an occasion is offered for baptizing it in human blood, the young brave who becomes its owner tries its quality on living animals, or, better still, on the corpses of criminals. When the executioner delivers to him the body, in accordance with higher authority, he fastens it to a cross, or upon trestles, in the court of his dwelling, and sets to work to cut, slash, and pierce, until he has acquired enough strength and skill to divide two bodies, one laid upon the other, at a single blow.

"We may easily imagine the aversion which these Japanese gentlemen, for whom the sabre is at once an emblem of their value and of their titles of nobility, feel for the fire-arms of the Western nations. The Tycoon formerly sent some of the young yakounins to Nagasaki, to learn the musketry drill from the Dutch officers there; but when they returned to the capital and were distributed among the barracks in order to drill the new Japanese infantry, their former comrades cried 'Treason!' and assailed them with arms in their hands. Nevertheless, the sabre is surely destined to become obsolete. In spite of the traditional prestige with which the privileged caste endeavors to surround it, in spite of the contempt which they affect for the military innovations of a government which they hate, the democratic weapon, the musket, is introduced into Japan, and with it, undoubtedly, a social revolution, which is already predicted in the instinctive but fruitless resistance of the representatives of the feudal spirit.

"The conduct of their chiefs will of itself tend to precipitate the catastrophe. Conspiracies and political assassinations increase at Yedo with a frightful rapidity. It appears to be settled that not only several Ministers of State, but two successive Tycoons, have perished by a violent death since the opening of Japan. The same fate overtook the *Gotairo*, or Regent, tutor of the young sovereign who died in 1866. His palace is seated on a hill in the southern part of the quarter of

Sakourada, fronting the broad moats and high walls of the inner circuit of the castle, and overlooking on the east and south, grand squares of streets formed by more than fifty seignorial residences. In this princely neighborhood, on the 24th of March, 1860, at eleven o'clock in the morning, the Regent, with an escort of four or five hundred men, was assailed by a band of seventeen *lonins* (bravos), on the spacious highway skirting the moat. There was sanguinary fighting on both sides; twenty soldiers of the escort fell at their posts; five conspirators were slain, two disemboweled themselves, four were made prisoners, and the others escaped, among them the chief, carrying the Regent's head in his mantle. Rumor added that the head was exposed in the provincial town where resides the Prince of Mito, the instigator of the conspiracy, then even at Miako, before the battlements of the Mikado, and finally that it was found in the Regent's own garden, where it had been thrown by night over the walls."

CHAPTER XII.

THE RESIDENCE OF THE TYCOONS.

"BY following the road which skirts the terraces of the Regent's palace, we finally reach a plateau on the northeastern side of the castle, the most elevated point being nearly on a level with the top of the interior glacis of the latter. The residence of the Tycoon appears to us to be seated on the southwestern extremity of the long chain of hills and plateaus which constitute the southern, western, and northern quarters of the capital.

"The undulating outlines of Yedo, from the southern side, present the image of a vast amphitheatre, the grades of which descend toward the bay. Hollows formed by the windings of three rivers may be traced through it, in the distance, the southernmost between Sinagawa and Takanawa; the second, between the latter quarter and those of Asabon and Atakosta; the nearest and most considerable between Atakosta and Sakourada, the same which fills the moats of the castle and the navigable canals of the commercial city, between the castle and the sea. Toward the east we see no summits; the city extends in a continuous plain to the great river Ogawa, beyond which the populous quarters of Hindjo are gradually lost in the mists of the horizon. All that part of Yedo to the eastward of the castle was entirely unknown to us, and, far as the view extended, we could not discover its end.

"The immensity of the Japanese capital produces a strange impression. The imagination, as well as the vision, is fatigued in hovering over that boundless agglomeration of human dwellings, all of which, great or little, are marked by the same stamp of uniformity. Each one of our old European cities has its distinctive physiognomy, strongly indicated by the monuments of different ages, and uniting to grand artistic effects the austere charm of ancient memories. But at Yedo, all things are of the same epoch, and in the same style; everything rests on a single fact, on a single political circumstance, — the foundation of the dynasty of the Tycoons.. Yedo is a wholly modern city, which seems to be waiting for its history and its monuments.

"Even the residence of the Tycoon, viewed from a distance, offers nothing remarkable except its dimensions, its vast circuit of terraces, supported by enormous walls of granite, its parks of magnificent shade, and its moats resembling quiet lakes, where flocks of aquatic birds freely sport in the water. That which chiefly strikes the senses, within the inclosures, is the grand scale to which everything is conformed: walls, avenues of trees, canals, portals, guard-houses, and dwellings of the retainers. The exquisite neatness of the squares and avenues, the profound silence which reigns around the buildings, the noble simplicity of these constructions of cedar upon marble basements, — all combine to produce a solemn effect, and to provoke those impressions of majesty, mystery, and fear, which despotism needs in order to support its prestige.

"Here, as in the Japanese temples, one cannot but admire the simplicity of the means employed by the native architects, in realizing their boldest conceptions. They always borrow the most effective of their resources directly from nature. The Tycoon's hall of audience possesses neither columns, nor statues, nor furniture of any kind. It consists of a succession of vast and very lofty chambers, separated one from the other by movable screens, which reach to the ceiling. They are so disposed as to give an effect of perspective, like the side-scenes of a theatre, and the end of the vista opens upon broad lawns and avenues of trees.

"The Tycoon's throne is a sort of dais, raised several steps, and supported against the wall which faces the principal entrance. The resident delegates of the Court of the Mikado, the Ministers of State, and the members of the Representative Council of the Daimios, have their seats on his right or left. Through the whole extent of the hall, as far as the eye can reach, the high court officials, the princes of feudal provinces, the lords of cities, castles, districts of the country, and the chiefs of the military aristocracy, are ranged by hundreds — or at the grand receptions, by thousands — in the places assigned to them by their rank in the hierarchy. No sound is heard in this immense crowd; each one is without arms, and barefooted, his feet concealed in the folds of immense dragging trousers. The daimios are recognized by their high-pointed caps and their long mantles of brocade, ornamented, on the sleeves, with the family coat-of-arms The officers of the Tocoon wear an **over-dress** of silken gauze, spreading out on the shoulders like two large wings.

"The assembly, divided into distinct groups, await the arrival of the Tycoon, crouched in silence on the thick bamboo matting which covers the floor. Then they prostrate themselves before the sovereign as soon as he appears, and until, seated on his throne, he has ordered his ministers to receive communications from the audience. Each orator or reporter prostrates himself anew on approaching the throne, and when commanded to speak. The costume of the Tycoon is composed of a robe of brocade with long sleeves, bound around the waist with silken cords, and large puffed trousers which cover his velvet boots. He wears on the top of his head a pointed hat of gold, which somewhat resembles the Doge's bonnet. What more splendid, or more majestic decoration could he give to his audience-hall, than this living gallery of the glories of Japan, this august assembly of princes, lords, and high officials, personifying the wealth and power of the Empire?

"This picture, which the Tycoon sees with so much pride, is the characteristic work of Iyeyas. It belongs to him especially, for it is not a continuation of the work of Taikosama. The latter was the last *Siogoon :* Iyeyas was the true founder of the dynasty of the *Tycoons.* It is true, however, that he never received such a designation; his illustrious name in the Japanese annals is Gonghensama. As to the title of Tycoon, its origin is modern, dating only from 1856. At this time, in one of the conferences of Commodore Perry with the representatives of the Japanese government at Yokohama, the American ambassador, wishing to designate in the treaty the political chief of the empire, and finding it difficult to choose between the titles, Siogoon, Konbosama, and others which the Mikados had conferred on their temporal lieutenants, the interpreter Hyashi proposed to adopt a uniform style, expressed by the two Chinese signs *Taï-Koun*, signifying 'Great Chief,' which was agreed upon by both sides. Since then, although the Japanese government has more than once expressed dissatisfaction with this innovation, it has been retained in all the international treaties, and has even become popular throughout the country.

"Before visiting the commercial city, and in order to finish with the official grandeurs of the capital, we must devote a few words to what is called the *Daimio-kodzi*, or Avenue of Princes. It stretches to the east and northeast of the Tycoon's palace, communicating with the quarter of Sourouga by five bridges, furnished with armed gateways. But it was not permitted to us to cross any of these. One was reserved for the Tycoon, another for Stotsbashi, and so on, until we reached a sixth, by which we were finally allowed to cross into the privileged zone.

"Here there are at least thirty heraldic palaces, and a great number of public edifices in the same style of architecture, such as the official residence of Stotsbashi; the office of the Prime Minister; of the Governor of the City, a personage whose influence with the ruler equals that of a favorite minister; of the Tycoon's architect, the man who occupies the next most enviable position at court; the hall of justice, with its gloomy dependencies, prisons, torture-rooms, and place of secret executions; finally the houses of the fire-brigade, store-houses of rice and bamboo matting for the castle. All this mass of residences and buildings for the use of the political administration of Japan has a stamp of simplicity and severity which is found in no other country. Within its limits, we must add, there are neither dwellings of citizens or of subordinate officials, temples, monasteries, tea-houses, theatres, or schools.

"The circuit which we were obliged to make, in order to enter the Daimio-kodzi, enabled us to see one of the largest military schools of the capital, although we did not succeed in entering the rooms devoted to study. We were allowed to see the fencing-halls; the riding-school, a vast oblong space, open to the sky, sanded and surrounded with a turfed bank; the stables, presenting the appearance of a long, low shed, with only a plank wall beside the mangers, where the horses were fed with chopped rice-straw; and finally the parade-ground, which was spacious enough to furnish practice for a battery of cannon, and which was often used for artillery maneuvres and target practice. These military schools are not regarded with much favor by the feudal aristocracy; but they are frequented as well by the sons of princes of the blood and the high officials of the empire as by those of the lower orders of the nobility, whose rank dates only from the favor of former Tycoons.

"One of the most remarkable departments of the University of Yedo is the college of interpreters. The numerous students who frequent it have the rank of officers and carry the two sabres. All are obliged to learn Dutch, which is the language of diplomatic relations, that in which the affairs of the Japanese government are arranged with foreign powers. After having acquired it, some add the English language; others Russian, others French, Portuguese, German, Danish, and even Italian, since Italy has also concluded a treaty with Japan, under the patronage of France. Thus, each one of the languages spoken by the contracting nations is represented at Yedo.

"Moriyama Yenoski was formerly the interpreter appointed to be present at all negotiations concerning the adoption or revision of international conventions. When I made his acquaintance, it appeared evident to me that he had been advanced in rank. He had occupied a confidential position with the Japanese embassies which visited the United States and Europe. I only saw him on two occasions, and then less as interpreter than as confidential assistant of the Minister of Foreign Affairs.

"Other interpreters have the special duty of selecting, translating, and annotating the newspapers which the court of the Tycoon receives directly from Europe, as well as the new scientific or literary works presented by the legations. All such publications are carefully preserved in the Imperial Library. By degrees materials are drawn from them for Japanese works, more or less extensive, written for the classes of civil and military officers, to whom they may be of service, or even for the public in general. We find already fragments of Humboldt's 'Cosmos,' an abridgment of Hufeland's 'Makrobiotik,' a translation of Stielier's Atlas, and of

Maury's work on 'Ocean Currents.' During the entire duration of the civil war in the United States, there was published in Yedo, at irregular intervals, a narration of events, accompanied with engravings on wood, copied from the American illustrated papers.

"We are far from being able to sound the mysteries of this Venice of the extreme East, and it must be difficult, even for the Japanese, to form a correct idea of it. But no one in Yedo is ignorant that the gloomy prisons in the Daimio-kodzi, the outside of which only we see, contain their torture-chambers, their dungeons, their places for secret executions.

"In Japan, the simple repression of common offenses is marked with ferocity, from beginning to end; the bloodhound of the police falls upon an accused person like a vulture on his prey. The bamboo is the necessary accompaniment of the examinations; the indictment is presented at length to the prisoner, and if he does not reply as the judge desires a rain of blows falls upon his shoulders. Woe to him, if he be suspected of lying, or of screening himself by denials! In such a case he is made to kneel upon pieces of hard wood, and in this position stone weights are piled upon his thighs until the blood gushes from the skin.

"In the eyes of a Japanese judge, the accused is always held to be guilty. The tribunal desires victims, and the police agents are its purveyors. Twenty to thirty prisoners are brought into the hall of justice at the same time; all wear the same costume, — a large mantle of blue cotton, and no other article of dress. As they are not allowed to shave or comb their hair, a few days are enough to give them the appearance of filthy creatures, for whom one would feel a sentiment of contempt or disgust. They sleep crouched upon the flag-stones with which the prison is paved; yet those who are able to pay may obtain from the jailer one or more mats and a wadded covering. Rice is their only food. The most absolute silence is imposed upon them, and this rule is only broken when one of their number has been condemned to death, and the soldiers come to carry him away. His companions are then allowed to utter, together and with all the strength of their voices, one long, despairing cry; after which the silence becomes more horrible than ever.

"The punishments provided by Japanese law are only imprisonment accompanied with corporeal inflictions, or death. Banishment is reserved for the grandees of the empire, or the bonzes, who are relegated, according to their rank, to one or the other outer islands. It is said that they spend the time of their exile in weaving silk stuffs. As to imprisonment, it is never of long duration, unless before the trial. The sentence generally adds a few weeks or months, as I have seen at Yokohama, where the valet of a European was condemned to a seclusion of three months for stealing. He was shut up with other malefactors in a high cell, — four whitewashed walls surmounted with a grating of heavy beams, — and received daily for his nourishment a bowl of rice and a *tempo* (about three cents), in exchange for which the jailer furnished him with a little fruit or vegetables.

"The theft of a less sum than forty *itzibus* (about twenty dollars), is punished by branding. In place of a hot iron, the Japanese make use of a lancet, with which they effect an incision of a certain form on the left arm, and make it indelible with powder. The prisoner thrusts his arm through a hole in the wall, and a surgeon in the next room performs the operation. The branding, in the case of a hardened criminal, may be repeated twenty-four times, but the last marks are then made upon the forehead, and every branding after the third is accompanied with a flogging.

"Every culprit who falls into the hands of justice after having been marked twenty-four times, or who commits a theft of greater amount than forty itzibus, is condemned to death. Ordinarily they wait until there are three or four to be executed, and the sentences are then carried into effect in the court-yard of the prison, with no other witnesses than the officers of justice. Each culprit is led into their presence, his eyes bandaged, and his *kirimon* thrown back upon his shoulders. He is made to kneel; four assistants, two on each side, grasp his hands and feet, and his head falls at a single stroke of the executioner's sword. It is then washed and exposed with the others in one of the market-places of the city, for twenty-four hours. The body is immediately stripped and washed, and put into a straw sack to be delivered, with the others, to the gentlemen who wish to practice their noble art as swordsmen.

"Only flagrant criminals, such as incendiaries and assassins, are executed in public. The former are given to the flames; the latter, where there is no aggravating circumstance, are beheaded. I might have seen in Yedo, the crucifixion of two parricides, for I received one morning from Tô, a paper containing an account of their crime and their approaching execution.

A PARRICIDE ON THE WAY TO EXECUTION.

"He had bought it from a colporteur who was crying his copies through the streets, as in the most civilized and Christian cities.

"As in Europe, the ceremonies of public executions are said to be for the purpose of making a salutary impression on the masses. The condemned is placed on horseback, bound to a high wooden saddle, and always has a rosary suspended to his neck. At the head of the procession the officers of justice direct the attention of the people to a large placard, borne by coolies, which relates in emphatic terms the circumstances of the crime.

"In all despotic States, the yoke of power always weighs most heavily on the *bourgeoisie*, — the class of untitled and unprivileged citizens. In Japan, this class is not yet formed, and only exists in reality in the Tycoon's cities, which are: Miako, Yedo, Hiogo, Osaka, Sakai, Nagasaki, and Hakodadi, to which may be added the new ports of Yokohama and Niagata. This very recent class of Japanese society bears in its breast the germs of the great future which seems to be marked out for the Japan of our day. Nevertheless, they do not yet exercise any civic right, and the lowest of the *hattamottos*, or small nobles, disdains to ally himself with the best family of the capital.

"The same spirit, fatal to progress, foreign to true civilization, hostile to humanity, reigns in the proud seats of the aristocracy and the government. The Tycoons have never been able to comprehend that the only real basis of their power, and the surest source of the prosperity of their empire, is found in this very class of simple citizens, which they have always crushed as in an iron cage."

CHAPTER XIII.

THE COURT AND ITS REVENUES.

O-SIRO, as the castle is properly called, situated very nearly in the centre of Yedo, is a sort of citadel, about five miles in circuit. It contains within it the palace of the Tycoon, of the presumptive heir, and of the principal members of the reigning family; but not in that circumstance alone consists its true grandeur. Even in despotic countries, the surroundings of a dynasty constitute its splendor. To appreciate the Tycoonal power — at least as it has been, — we must have a correct idea of the court which sustains it. The following statistics are partly drawn from the annual reports published in Yedo and partly from Dutch sources. The historic accounts of the families, or biographical sketches of the most important personages, cannot be given, since the materials have not yet been collected.

The estimate of the revenues, or annual salaries of the principal functionaries of the government, however, is taken from the official reports of the government and may be fully relied on. All salaries belonging to public employment in Japan, are paid in, or at least calculated according to, products, — that is, *kokous*, or sacks of rice, each of which has a weight of about one hundred English pounds, and a value of about $3.25.

THE COURT AND ITS REVENUES.

The following table, therefore, very nearly represents the revenues of the Japanese court: —

1. The first dignitary of the court is the Regent, or Gotairo, whose office is hereditary in the house of Kamon-no-Kami. The annual revenue of this office is $1,080,000.

2. The second is the representative of the Tycoon at the court of the Mikado. Annual salary, $320,000.

3. The Council of Daimios, composed of eighteen representatives of the eighteen great feudal lords, each of whom receives annually from $100,000 to $240,000.

4. The members of the Council of State, or Council of Ministers, five in number. They are generally officials belonging to the secondary nobility, and of small property. Each receives about $170,000.

5. The second Council of State, or Administrative Council, with five to thirteen members, heads of the various departments of government, each from $40,000 to $160,000.

6. The Adjutant-general and Grand Messenger of the State, a prince of the second or third class, $140,000.

7. Aids-de-camp in ordinary service, sixteen in number, from $6,000 to $16,000.

8. Ambassadors to the feudal lords, from whom are chosen the members of the embassies sent to Europe and America, twenty in number, from $3,200 to $10,000.

9. Princes charged with the military defense of the domains of the Tycoon, twenty to thirty feudal lords of the second and third class. Their salaries (which oblige them to furnish a certain number of

men, who are at the disposal of the government) vary from $50,000 to $280,000.

10. Princes with various military commands, twenty-five in number, averaging $58,000.

11. Princes, commanding fortresses of the Tycoon, twelve in number, with from $9,500 to $32,000.

12. Princes attached to embassies, etc., four to eight, from $6,000 to $20,000.

13. Princes appointed to superintend the chief police arrangements, especially the administration of the temples, four, from $140,000 to $200,000.

14. Chamberlains, twelve to twenty, $20,000.

15. Chancellors of State, five, $10,000.

16. Governors of Yedo, two, $10,000.

17. Governors of the Treasury, four, $5,000.

18. Governor of Public Works, architect and engineer, $5,000.

19. Governors of the Navy, two, $8,000.

20. Heralds of arms, three, $14,000 to $26,000.

21. Commanders of body-guards, four, $16,000.

22. Generals: one hundred to one hundred and twenty, from $1,200 to $24,000.

23. Inspector General of the Armories, $16,000.

24. Governors of cities, etc., twenty, $2,800 to $6,000.

In this estimate the hundreds, nay, the thousands of subordinate officials who complete the administration of the Tycoon's government are not included.

The salaries which have been designated amount to very near $24,000,000 annually, and $30,000,000 would probably not be an over-estimate for the entire expense which the Japanese government entails upon the people.

Soto-siro is the general term which comprises the quarters surrounding the castle. Their limits are the outer circle of moats, the canals which communicate with the Ogawa, and the great river itself, on the east. In its entire extent, the Soto-siro has a circumference of a little less than ten miles. It embraces both the quarters of the nobility and the commercial part of the city on the right bank of the Ogawa River. The part appropriated by the nobility is divided into four districts: that called Sakourada is almost entirely taken up by the mansions of the princes. There are no burghers' dwellings except along the main highway which traverses it. Here, in this more elevated region, are the residences of the families related to the Tycoon, the three branches of Ksiou, Owari, and Mito. The Regent's palace is distinguished by its grand dimensions, and its picturesque situation, beside the second moat.

More than a hundred palaces of the first, second, and third class cover the plain behind the temple of Sanno, in these quarters, and in several others, generally formed by large square tracts, surrounded by broad sanded avenues.

CHAPTER XIV.

THE CITIZENS' QUARTER.

"IT was not long," says M. Humbert, " before I received a first warning. The government deigned to inform me that our extensive excursions through the capital might result in danger to ourselves. There was no further time to lose, for they were evidently preparing obstacles to our movements. I calculated that we had already traversed about one third of the thirty districts into which the city is divided; a new, and perhaps a final field of exploration must be immediately selected from the remainder.

"It seemed to me that the greatest number of objects of interest, were included within a circle having the chief bridge of the city for its central point. The latter could be speedily reached, either on horseback by the Tokaïdo, or in a boat, taking advantage of the tide; and it was but a short distance further to the populous quarters of the commercial city, on the right bank of the Ogawa, or to the industrial city of Hondjo, on the left bank.

"I had already made out a programme of our expeditions, when an amusing adventure occurred, which encouraged me in my plans, and at the same time showed me their true value. Two attachés of the Prussian Legation at Yokohama came to visit M. Met-

A JAPANESE STABLE.

man, and as they wished to procure both the Almanac of the Mikado's Court, and the official Annual of the Tycoon's government, the latter gentleman accompanied them to the shop of a bookseller in the city. I begged him to purchase for me at the same time, any literary curiosities or specimens of native art which might fall into his hands.

"When the gentlemen, together with their yakounins, were installed in the bookstore, the owner at once furnished them with the 'Almanac of Miako,' which was on hand. He stated that the 'Yedo Annual' was also to be had, and, pushing aside a screen, entered the next room. One of the yakounins accompanied him; presently the two returned, the bookseller stammering out that he had no 'Annuals' to sell. 'Well,' said one of the Prussian secretaries, 'send to another shop for them; we will wait here.' Thereupon there was a movement among the yakounins, consultations in the street, and prolonged absence of the bookseller. During this time the three strangers lighted their cigars, and asked an employé of the establishment to bring them boxes to sit upon, and to place before them all the illustrated works in the shop. When the owner returned, he bowed to the ground, and sighed out: 'The "Annual" cannot be had in the neighborhood, and it is now too late to send to the castle.'

"'What of that?' was the reply. 'Send your boy for it! For our part, we are going to have our dinner brought here; we shall not leave you until we have the "Annual."'

"M. Metman thereupon wrote a note, which he sent

to the steward of the Legation by one of the men of the escort. The bookseller also gave a commission to one of his employés, and the review of illustrated works was continued until the arrival of four coolies, carrying at the extremity of their bamboo poles, the lacquered boxes and wicker baskets containing the dinner.

"The meal was spread upon the matting; the yakounins and the bookseller were invited to take part in it, but they politely declined. Nevertheless, when the sound of champagne corks began to be heard, they drew nearer, and the foaming glasses soon circulated around the shop. 'Have you anything more to show us by way of dessert?' asked M. Metman.

"The bookseller answered: 'You already know the contents of my shop. I have nothing more to show except some drawings, sketches on detached sheets, made by two artists of Yedo, lately deceased. It is all which they have left to their families, who have given me the useless legacy for a small supply of rice. Here are still the old sheets on which they tried their pencils. If you like the sketches, take the package along with the books you have bought.'

"M. Metman called the coolies, and ordered them to fill their baskets with the dishes, the packages of books and drawings; but to leave the bottles and the remainder of the dinner for the yakounins and the people of the house. Then, turning to the bookseller, he said: 'Will it be necessary, do you think, to order our mattresses and quilts, in order to pass the night here? Now is the time to send for them by the coolies.'

"A general hilarity succeeded this question; then

there were whisperings and goings to and fro, between
the shop and the street, where an increasing crowd of
curious spectators endeavored to find out what strange
drama was being enacted. At last the owner and his
employé reappeared, bearing some volumes under their
arms. He bowed again, and placed in the hands of
the strangers, evidently with the consent of the yakounins, two perfectly authentic copies of the official 'Annual of Yedo.'

"I passed the night in examining the precious collection. It was composed of thirty illustrated works
and a quantity of sheets, loose or sewed together.
Here were old encyclopædias, enriched with plates
which seemed to have issued from the German work-
shops of the Middle Ages; there, albums of sketches
in India ink, reproduced on wood, or collections of
stories and popular scenes, illustrated with pictures
in two tints, produced by a process unknown to us.
Numerous paintings on silk and rice paper represented
the bridges, the markets, the theatres, all the places of
meeting, and all the types of the laboring classes and
the burgher society of Yedo. But nothing of all these
equaled in importance the posthumous work of the
two poor unknown artists, for the latter revealed to me
both the favorite subjects and the style of the modern
school of Japanese painters. These sketches, inspired
by the scenes of the streets and public gardens, were
a veritable treasure for the study of the people of
Yedo. These dusty and spotted bundles, wherein I
found a hundred and two finished pictures and a hundred and thirty rough sketches, devoted exclusively to
the classes which live outside of the Castle, the aristo-

cratic quarters, the barracks and the monasteries, were a mine to be worked! Such a collection was for me the surest guide, the most faithful interpreter which I could have consulted, before plunging into the labyrinth of streets, quays, and canals which thread the masses of the dwellings of the *bourgeoise* population, on both sides of the river.

"The district of Nipon-bassi, or the Bridge of Nipon, which is the heart of the city, contains in a space of four square kilometres, five longitudinal, and twenty-two cross streets, cutting the former at right angles, and forming seventy-eight blocks of houses, each being almost the exact model of the other. Navigable canals surround this long parallelogram on the four sides, and fifteen bridges give it communication with the other parts of the city. Although they have a character so completely homogeneous, these quarters of the city do not leave that impression of fastidious monotony which the mansions belonging to the court or the feudal nobility rarely fail to produce. The houses of the citizens, not less than the palaces, do not vary from the type of architecture which is appropriate to them: they are simple constructions of wood, but two stories in height, the upper one bordered by a gallery looking upon the street, with a low roof covered with slate-colored tiles, and having plaster ornaments at the extremities of the ridge-pole. But if the frame be the same, the pictures which it incloses are delightful in their variety, unexpectedness, and picturesque originality.

"Here at the entrance of a street of Nipon-bassi, there is a barber's shop, where three citizens, in the simplest apparel, come to make their morning toilette.

Seated on stools, they gravely hold up with the left hand the lacquered dish which receives the spoils of the razor or scissors. The artists, on their side, relieved of everything which may restrict the freedom of their movements, bend to the right or left of their customers' heads, which they traverse with hand or instrument, like ancient sculptors modeling caryatides.

"A few steps further, we find a shoemaker's shop. It bristles with wooden hooks, from which hang innumerable pairs of straw sandals. The owner, squatted on his counter, reminds me of one of those native idols, to which the pilgrims make offerings of shoes. Persons of both sexes stop in front of him, examine the sandals or try them on, exchange some friendly words with him, and lay the proper price at his feet without disturbing him.

"Then follow shops for the sale of sea-weed, several varieties of which are cooked and eaten by the people. There is also, in Yedo, an enormous consumption of shell-fish. Oysters are abundant and fleshy, but not very delicate; the Japanese have no other way of opening them except to break the upper shell with a stone. At Uraga a large species of oyster is dried and exported to all parts of the empire; the trade therein is said to be a royalty of the Tycoon.

"The show of the seed-stores of Yedo is very attractive. The quantity and infinite variety of the products offered, the diversity of their forms and colors, the art with which they are arranged on the shelves, all combine to attract the attention; but we are filled with surprise and admiration on perceiving that each one of the packages already enveloped in paper, each one of the cones ready for sale, bears, with the name of the seed, a sketch in colors of the plant itself. The illustration is often a little masterpiece, which seems to have been stolen from some charming floral album. We soon discover the artist and his studio,— that is, some young workman of the establishment, stretched at full length upon mats sprinkled with flowers and sheets of paper, and in this singular attitude making every touch of his brush produce the true effect.

"As we approach the central bridge of the district the crowd increases, and on both sides of the street the shops give place to popular restaurants, to pastry-shops of rice and millet, and the sale of tea and hot saki. Here we are in the neighborhood of the great fish market. The canal is covered with boats, which land fresh sea-fish and the product of the rivers, the fish of the polar currents and those of the equatorial stream, tortoises of the bay of Nipon, deformed polypi, and fantastic crustacea. Siebold counted, in this market-place, seventy different varieties of fish, crabs, and mollusks, and twenty-six kinds of mussels and other shell-fish.

"The stalls, roughly erected near the landing-place, are besieged by purveyors who come to purchase at the auctions. Amid the tumultuous throngs vigorous arms are seen lifting the heavy baskets and emptying them into the lacquered boxes of the coolies; from time to time the crowd gives way to let two coolies pass, carrying a porpoise, a dolphin, or a shark, suspended by cords to a bamboo across their shoulders. The Japanese boil the flesh of these animals; they even salt down the blubber of whales.

JAPANESE COOK.

" Toward the middle of the day, during the hot season, the streets of Yedo become deserted; the shores of the canals are lined with empty boats, fastened to the piles. No clamor, no noise comes up from the depths of the great city. If we still distinguish, here and there, either a traveller or a couple of pilgrims, hurrying along to reach their midday resting-place, they walk in silence, with bowed heads and eyes fatigued with the glare of the road. The rays of the sun make broad luminous zones, whereon are drawn the outlines of the shadows which fall from broad roofs upon the flag-stones of the pavements, or from centenary trees upon the turf of the gardens.

" The population of the streets and canals is withdrawn within the hostelries or private dwellings, where, in the remote basement rooms, they enjoy the principal meal of the day, and then give two or three hours to sleep. In pursuing our route from street to street, along the shaded sidewalks, the eye looks through the openings between the screens, detects the household interiors, and catches glimpses of picturesque groups of men, women, and children, squatted around their simple dinner.

" The table-cloth, made of woven straw, is spread upon the floor matting. In the centre is placed a great bowl of lacquered wood, containing rice, which is the basis of food with all classes of Japanese society. The usual manner of preparing it, is to place it in a small keg of very light wood, which is then dropped into a kettle of boiling water. Each guest attacks the common supply, taking as much rice as will fill and heap a large porcelain bowl, which he sets to his lips, eating without the use of chop-sticks until the supply is nearly exhausted, when he adds to the rice some pieces of fish, crabs, or fowls, taken from the dish appropriated to animal food. The meats are seasoned with sea-salt, pepper, and soy, a very pungent sauce produced by the fermentation of a variety of black beans. Soft or hard eggs, cooked vegetables, such as turnips, carrots, sweet potatoes, pickles made of sliced bamboo sprouts, and a salad made of the bulbous roots of the lotus, complete the bill of fare of an ordinary Japanese dinner.

"Tea and saki are necessary accompaniments, both being generally taken hot and without sugar. I have never examined the beautiful utensils of a Japanese meal,— their bowls, cups, saucers, boxes, wooden plates, their porcelain urns, cups, and flagons, their tea-pots of glazed porous earthenware; and I have never watched the guests at the table, with the grace of their movements and the dexterity of their small and elegant hands, without fancying them to be a company of large children, playing at housekeeping, and eating for amusement rather than to satisfy their appetites. The diseases resulting from excess at the table or an unwholesome diet are generally unknown; but the immoderate use of their national drink, frequently gives rise to serious disorders. I myself saw more than one case of delirium tremens.

"Notwithstanding the ease with which Yedo might be supplied with excellent water, the people are almost entirely dependent on cisterns. From this cause, and the recklessness with which they eat unripe fruit, the cholera and dysentery make great ravages among them. Their popular hygiene prescribes little except hot baths.

JAPANESE RESTAURANT AT YEDO.

which they take every day. This passion for cleanliness, the salubrity of their climate, the excellent character of their aliment, ought to make the Japanese the most healthy and robust people in the world. Nevertheless, there are few races more afflicted with all sorts of cutaneous affections, and certain forms of chronic and incurable disease, the cause of which cannot certainly be found in the natural conditions of their lives.

"There are a great many physicians in Japan, and especially at Yedo. Those attached to the court of the Tycoon belong to the class of small nobles, wearing two sabres, shaving the head, and possessing a rank more or less elevated, according to their official standing. The first, limited in number, comprises the physicians attached to the house of the sovereign, who have no practice outside of the palace. The fees which they receive, in money or supplies, represent an annual income of from three to four thousand dollars. Those of the second category are the officers of health, attached to the army in time of war, who receive a salary of about two thousand dollars. When they are not in service, they occasionally practice in private families. The members of both classes are appointed by the government.

"As there are no examinations required for the practice of medicine, each one adopts the profession at will and practices according to his own method. Some retain the routine of the native quacks; others treat their patients according to the rules of Chinese medical art; others, again, acquire a smattering of European ideas, through the Dutch. The wish of the people is to have plenty of physicians in case of need, and to be dosed according to three systems at once, rather than a single good one.

"The Japanese doctors are easily recognized by their severe air, their measured gait, and several curious peculiarities, which they appear to adopt purposely, according to their fancy. I have seen them with the head shaven like a priest, with long locks rounded at the neck, or even with a flowing beard. In this manner they acquire a general consideration among the people, and are often, especially in the houses of the aristocracy, paid rather by external forms of respect than by dollars. Such, indeed, are the conditions of life in most families, that, toward the end of the year, after having met all the indispensable expenses, including family festivals, the theatre, baths, priests, and excursions of pleasure, there remains very little for the doctor. Nevertheless, the latter philosophically accepts the situation. He often exhibits a genuine disinterestedness, and a zeal in the exercise of his profession, which presumes a passion for science ; and it is not too much to say that the Japanese physicians will probably be among the first to contribute to the progress of civilization in their country.

"The Dutch physicians, within the past fifteen years, have successfully introduced vaccination at Nagasaki, and the use of anatomical models into the medical school at Mikado. In September, 1859, Doctor Van Meerdervort, having obtained the necessary authority from the Tycoon, assembled forty-five Japanese physicians on a promontory of the harbor of Nagasaki, and from eight in the morning until sunset dissected the body of a culprit who had been executed. There was considerable excitement among the people, but the governor allayed it by issuing the following proclamation: 'Considering that the body of the malefactor has been of service to medical science, and consequently to the public good, the government undertakes to provide, within twenty-four hours, honorable burial for the remains of the criminal, with the coöperation of the ministers of religion.'"

CHAPTER XV.

THE BRIDGES OF YEDO. — THE POLICE.

"OF all the great cities of the world, Yedo seems to me the most favored by nature, in regard to situation, climate, richness of vegetation, and abundance of running water. It is seated at the mouth of two rivers, one of which washes the eastern side of the Hondjo, and the other, traversing from north to south the most populous quarters of the city, separates the Hondjo from the latter and from the two suburbs of Asaksa.

"Basins with locks, ponds, moats, a complete network of navigable canals, connect the natural courses of the rivers, and carry to the heart of the city proper, as well as to all parts of the Hondjo, the movements of commerce and life throughout the immense capital.

"Among the numerous canals which radiate from the moats of the castle, the most important is that which is spanned by the famous Bridge of Nipon. From the summit of this bridge, which is a high arch, the most picturesque view of Yedo may be obtained. Looking toward the south, we see on the horizon the white pyramid of Fusi-yama; on the right the city is dominated by the terraces, parks, and square towers of the residence of the Tycoon. In the same direction, as far as its junction with the moats of the castle, the canal of Nipon-bassi is lined, on both sides, with storehouses of silk, cotton, rice, and saki. To the left, beyond the fish-market, the view is lost among the streets and canals leading toward the Ogawa River. Hundreds of long barks, transporting wood, charcoal, bamboo canes, matting, covered baskets, boxes, barrels, or large fish, thread the navigable ways in all directions, while the streets seem to be exclusively given up to the circulation of the people. From time to time, it is true, we distinguish among the crowds of pedestrians a drove of horses or of black buffaloes, heavily laden, the latter wearing double strings of bells over their flanks; or two-wheeled carts, whereupon four or five tiers of bales and boxes are artistically piled, drawn by coolies. No other sound of wheels is heard; the noise of wooden sandals on the sidewalks, and the reverberating bridges, the confused sounds from the canals, with the bells of the buffaloes, and the measured cries of the coolies, form altogether a strange harmony, which has no resemblance to the voice of any other city. For each of the great capitals has its own peculiar tongue. In London it is the hollow roar of a rising tide; in Yedo, the murmur of the retiring wave.

"The harbor for junks is at the mouth of the large river. The population, on both banks, is essentially plebeian. With the exception of some mansions of the second and third class, these quarters are filled with the dwellings of fishermen, mariners, mechanics, and small tradesmen. The great bridge of Yetai, the squares, and neighboring streets are constantly enlivened with crowds of people, the greater part of whom seem to have no other object than recreation.

"There are no less than four enormous bridges thrown across the river, at nearly regular intervals of from twenty to thirty minutes' walk, and the open squares abutting them, on both shores, are equally spacious. The O-bassi, or Great Bridge, is about three hundred and fifty yards in length, and rests, like all the others, on some twenty piers, each formed of three transverse piles, strongly connected by cross-pieces. Another bridge, of sixteen piers, communicates with the northern suburb of Inaka, with its orchards, villages, and rustic tea-houses. It is a region of rich culture, and charming landscapes; and the favorite resort of the citizens, for their picnics and family parties.

"The third bridge from the bay may be considered as the centre of the nocturnal recreations of the citizens and the small nobles. The great river, at this point, is not deep enough for the trading junks; but its surface is so broad that hundreds of light craft have room to ply in all directions. During the serene nights of summer, rafts laden with fireworks float along the stream and send towards heaven their sheaves of rockets and clusters of fiery stars. Gondolas, hung with lanterns of brilliant colors, glide around, or pass from one shore to another; while the larger barks, all garlanded with flags and lanterns, go up and down with merry companies, and the sound of guitars and songs. It is the very picture of a Venetian festival, only with different decorations. The large boats, however, generally belong to the proprietors of tea-houses, who rent them by the hour to families, or social companies, furnishing also the refreshments and music.

"The neighborhood of the bridges, far from injuring the effect of these simple concerts, rather adds to them a special charm. Seated at the threshold of a tea-house, near the middle bridge, we may easily pass several hours, indulging in the Japanese idleness, with the sound of song, and the tinkling of musical instruments rising above the murmurs of the crowd. In the intervals of silence we can hear the distant noise of the multitudes crossing the long wooden structures. No rolling of wheels, none of the discordant clamors of European cities come to break the charm of the impression. In Europe, indeed, only Venice gives the same movement of the people, the same mixture of footsteps, voices, songs, and music, which yet do not disturb the feeling of revery. The Ogawa River recalls the Grand Canal, and the vicinity of the chief bridges of Yedo, like the public squares of Venice, are the rendezvous of the population.

"As to the musical enjoyments of the Japanese, I must confess that they can only be appreciated by native ears. Their melodies have something strange, something which we cannot seize. The musical theory upon which they are based is not yet known; Japanese music is very rich in semitones, possibly in quarter-tones. Their musical instruments are also distinguished by their originality. Those with strings are made of the light and resonant wood of the *Paulownia imperialis*, and the strings of fine silk, covered with a light coating of lacquer. The chief instruments are the *samsin*, a species of guitar with three strings, and the *gotto*, something between a harp and a cither, with thirteen strings.

"Among the contrasts which Japanese society offers, there is one which manifests itself with a sort of perverse fatality, in almost all the streets of Yedo. On one side, there is the orderly aspect of the city, on the other, the barbarity of manners revealed by a certain class of official arrangements. Thus, while admiring the excellent condition of the squares, promenades, and ways of communication, the orderly character of the markets, and the movement of the crowds, all at once we are disagreeably surprised to find in advance, or or turning the angle of a street, a high and heavy barrier of wood, painted black, like a hideous indication of some scene of trouble, or violence, behind it. These barriers, which are guarded by the agents of the Tycoon, have a great central gate and two side doors, open during the day, as least so long as order is preserved, but regularly closed at nine or ten o'clock at night. Those who are out late are obliged to pull the cord beside one of these doors, and to answer such questions as the chief yakounin of the post may address to them through a wicket. The citizen is allowed to pass through the side-door, but the central portal is opened wide for a nobleman.

"By day, when the police wish to make arrests, domiciliary visits, to intervene in a street tumult, or to give succor in case of some serious accident, they commence by isolating the theatre of their operations, by closing these barriers.

"Coarse manners and boisterous habits characterize the coolies, the boatmen, and the grooms of the lower city, on the banks of the Ogawa River. They are never without fierce quarrels and rivalries. In certain cases they agree upon certain harmless trials of strength, the most original of which is carried out upon one of the arched bridges over the canals. The large cable of a junk is drawn from one shore to another over the span of the bridge; the members of each party then take hold of the ends. As soon as the signal has been given by the judges posted on the middle of the bridge, hundreds of muscular arms begin to pull, and with their whole strength in opposite directions. The rope grows taut, stretches, remains motionless and quivering, until finally one of the parties, yielding to fatigue, lets go suddenly, giving up the contest. The great attraction of the struggle is in this final catastrophe, which covers the earth with a crowd of combatants, tumbled pell-mell over each other. But it is still better when the cable suddenly breaks, and both parties, without the exception of a single man, bite the dust at the same time, uttering a general groan. To the hollow sound of their fall succeed endless clamors, an indescribable confusion, a vortex of men who scramble to their feet, withdraw, give themselves up to paroxysms of mad hilarity, meet their rivals on the bridge, and go together to the neighboring tea houses, to drink a general reconciliation in cups of saki.

"It is a part of the policy of the Japanese government to exercise a great deal of indulgence toward the passions of the people. One of the oldest European residents at Nagasaki informed me that he had seen, from the balcony of a native restaurant, a veritable pitched battle between the inhabitants of two neighboring streets. Both parties had inherited mutual hatred from their fathers, and had long lived in a condition of the bitterest enmity. The feeling finally grew to an outbreak; both sides armed themselves with bamboo sticks, arranged themselves in lines, and with loud cries began the battle. The police were soon upon the spot, but they contented themselves with closing the black barriers all around the field of conflict to prevent interruption, and for two hours allowed the fight to go on. At the end of that time, the governor of the city, satisfied that he was fulfilling the secret wish of both parties, sent agents commanding them to withdraw to their respective streets, which they did at once, without the least objection !

"In proportion as the field of my studies and observations increased, furnishing each day some new cause of satisfaction, it became evident that our relations with the authority in the castle of Yedo grew more difficult and uncertain. There were certain indications which led us to believe that a rupture between Japan and England was imminent. The feudal party prayed for this, and even solicited the Tycoon to order the indiscriminate expulsion of all foreigners. Menaces had even been uttered against the reigning dynasty, in the Council of Daimios. A nocturnal encounter in which the people of the castle were victorious, was the subject of mysterious conversations among our yakounins, and we had reason to believe that a celebrated chief of the *lonins*, or bravos, had been left upon the field.

"In spite of extraordinary precautions taken by the guard of the Legation, we determined to employ the remainder of our time — feeling confident that our residence in Yedo would soon come to an end — in completing, as far as might be possible, our survey of the city and its curiosities. It appeared to us, from the unusual agitation of the courtiers, who came to us every morning to offer their services, that they had received some secret counsel from our own guard or from the police. Fatigued with the annoyance, we dismissed them, and made ourselves excursions among the shops. We visited all that part of the city south of the bridge of Yedo, while a part of our company passed over to the left bank of the great river, and traversed on horseback the principal quays and most populous streets of the Hondjo. During these interesting trips, which were not disturbed by any disagreeable incident, we so completely forgot the state of siege in which we lived at the Tjoodji, that on returning it was hard to preserve a grave countenance, and not to mistake our guards, clad in helmets and preposterous armor, for knights escaped from the French comic opera.

"An interpreter of the Tycoon, named Kasuda Geogiro, who published at Yokohama, in July, 1869, seven letters relating to the internal troubles of Japan during the seven previous years, affirms that the measures taken by the government in 1863, both for the protection of the foreign legations, and for its own security, were not inspired by any chimerical fears. The southern princes, in leaving their mansions in Yedo, left behind them bands of bravos secretly organized for the purpose of defying, harassing, and weakening the central power: political assassinations, arson, conspiracies against foreigners, and acts of violence committed on the merchants who had commercial relations with Yokohama, were the means by which they endeavored to bring about a revolution of the feudal provinces."

CHAPTER XVI.

THE HONDJO.

"THE long eastern portion of Yedo, which covers the left bank of the river Ogawa, comprises three quarters. That of Sumidagawa, on the north, belongs to the suburbs, and presents an entirely rustic character. It is covered with rice-fields, kitchen gardens, vast horticultural establishments, and tea-houses, spread along the river or scattered in the rear of great orchards of pear, plum, peach, and cherry trees. The other two quarters, between the former and the bay, contain a dense population, composed, for the most part, of fishers, seamen, mechanics, and tradesmen. Thus the Hondjo proper corresponds to the industrial quarters of our large cities. We find there manufactures of tiles and coarse pottery, of cooking utensils of iron, paper-mills, establishments for cleaning and preparing cotton, domestic spinneries of cotton and silk, dyeing establishments and others for weaving mats, baskets, or cloth stuffs.

"Japanese industry does not yet make much use of machinery. Nevertheless, in the iron-foundries one frequently sees bellows driven by water, which is carried to the wheel in bamboo pipes. Both charcoal and stone-coal are used for the furnaces. Women have their share in all the industrial professions, which are usually carried on at home. There are no large manufactories in Japan: the members of the laboring class stay at home and carry on their occupations, which they interrupt in order to eat when they are hungry, and to rest whenever they please. In a company of six workmen of both sexes, there are almost always to be seen two smoking pipes and enlivening the toil of their comrades by merry speeches. Thus is developed, and transmitted from generation to generation that social instinct, that fund of good-humor and spirit of repartee which characterize the lower classes of the capital.

"The quarters of the Hondjo are constructed on a plan of the most perfect regularity. They are bounded on the south by the bay, on the west by the Ogawa River, on the east by a smaller river, and on the north by a canal which separates them from the suburb of Sumidagawa. Two canals traverse them from north to south, and three from east to west. The squares, thus formed, inclose a world totally different from that upon the opposite bank of the river. The Hondjo has no commercial life; it has neither the imposing masses of residences of the Castle, nor the animation of the places reserved for the pleasure of the populace in the northern quarters; nevertheless, we find there, existing under special conditions, commerce and industry, temples, palaces, and places of public resort. Some of the most important merchants of Japan reside in the Hondjo, but they have their places of business in the vicinity of the great bridges.

"The comparative tranquillity of this region beyond the river and the facility with which concessions of large tracts of ground are there obtained, seems to have favored the establishment of numerous monasteries, some of which possess large temples. There are forty of these sacred edifices, two of which are devoted to the ancient national worship, another, more than two hundred feet in length, to the Buddhist faith, and another dedicated to the Five Hundred Genii. One of the monasteries is celebrated for engaging, twice a year, all the chief wrestlers of Yedo, who give a series of public performances, — a pious speculation, which never fails to attract to the great lawn in front of the monastery an enormous crowd, made up of all classes of society. Thus, each temple or monastery has its own form of advertisement, and is distinguished by some singularity, — such as the avenue of statues of pigs, each nobly installed on a pedestal of granite, which we find on approaching one of the temples. Public opinion appears to accept without difficulty whatever device may be pleasing to the bonzes, without regard to its character.

"A certain number of families of the old nobility have made of the Hondjo a sort of Faubourg St. Germain, where they live in a profound retirement, far from the noises of the city and protected from contact with the world of the court, and the officers of the government. There, the walls of the Castle no longer offend the eyes of the fierce daimio. From the summits of the bridges arched over the canals, the grand alleys of trees around the Tycoon's residence, seen over the innumerable roofs of the merchant city, resemble the peaceful shades of some distant park, blended with the hills around the base of Fusi-yama.

PRIEST OF THE HIGHER GRADE.

"There are many workshops of sculpture in the Hondjo. I have never seen the artists working in marble, although there are quarries of it in the mountains of the interior. The pedestals of idols are made of granite, the candelabra of the sacred places, tombs, statuettes, Buddhist saints, and holy foxes, of a very fine sandstone. The wood-carvers make domestic altars of rich network, elegant caskets, elephants' heads, and monstrous chimeras for the roofs of temples, woodwork and mosaics representing cranes, geese, bats, mythologic animals, the moon half veiled by a cloud, branches of cedars, pines, bamboos, and palms. The idols, frequently of gigantic size, which are made in the workshops of Yedo, are generally surrounded by an aureole gilded and painted in lively colors: the guardians of heaven, for example, in vermilion, and others in indigo.

"Several interesting branches of industry are connected with that of the ebony-carvers. The framework of movable presses or screens is required to be ornamented with large drawings in India ink, executed by a few strokes of the pencil, or groups of trees and flowers of brilliant colors, or paintings of birds selected for the brilliance of their plumage. All this is done by hand, in the workshops. The embroidresses furnish for the fire-screens and curtains exquisite works, where the silk, under the patient labor of the needle, reproduces, according to the choice of subjects, the lustrous texture of leaves, the velvet down of birds, the tufted fur of animals, or the shining scales of fishes. Then the braiders of silk floss add to the luxury of the wood

11

work a decoration of garlands and knots of various colors, surmounted by groups of flowers and birds.

"The *obi*, a girdle which is worn by all adult Japanese women, married or single, with the exception of the ladies of princely families, is the article of feminine costume which presents the most variety, according to the taste or fancy of individuals. Sometimes it is very simple, sometimes remarkable for the richness of the stuff or the splendor of the embroideries. It is generally broad enough to serve at the same time as girdle and corset. It is wound around the body like a bandage, and fastened at the back by interlacing the ends so as to produce a large, flat furbelow, falling on the hips, or floating with a graceful negligence. A widow, who has determined not to marry again, knots the *obi* in front, and the same arrangement is adopted for female corpses.

"It is not an easy thing to penetrate into the Japanese workshops, especially under the surveillance of a squad of yakonnins. In spite of the promises of the latter, I was not able to see either the process of coloring, or the manufacture of rich silk stuffs, or of paper. On the other hand, I have always found both the wholesale and retail shops accessible even to the rear chamber, where one should never refuse to penetrate; for the Japanese merchant takes no trouble to display his stock. He prefers to keep his best goods in reserve, as if to give his purchasers the satisfaction of discovering them. In order to form a tolerable idea of the richness, the variety, and the artistic merit of Japanese industry, we must not only traverse the commercial streets frequented by the natives, but also imitate the latter in returning day by day to the same merchant, until we have explored every corner of his shop. This is the more necessary, since there is no general bazaar, each magazine or shop having its specialty.

"Certain forms of industry are as yet but little developed, among others saddlery, which will be discouraged as long as a religious prejudice exists against tanners and curriers. This circumstance renders Japan tributary to foreign countries, especially since the Tycoon and the princes rival each other in zeal for the reform of the cavalry and artillery. They import leather from England, and saddles and harness from Holland and France. Nevertheless, I noticed in Yedo a great variety of articles, of leather, tawed skins and shagreen, such as trunks and travelling satchels, portfolios, money bags, tobacco-pouches, and hunting-gloves, all of **native manufacture.**"

CHAPTER XVII.

JAPANESE ART AND INDUSTRY.

"WHATEVER may be the variety of industrial products displayed in the shops of the commercial city, there is one feature which characterizes all of them, one common stamp which denotes their place among the works of the far East, and I venture to call it, without fear of contradiction, good taste.

"The artisan of Yedo is a veritable artist. If we except the conventional style to which he still feels himself compelled to submit, in his representations of the human figure, if we overlook the insufficiency of his knowledge of the rules of perspective, we shall have only praise left for him in all other respects. His works are distinguished from those of Miako by the simplicity of his forms, the severity of the lines, the sobriety of the decorations, and the exquisite feeling for nature which he exhibits in all subjects of ornamentation drawn from the vegetable or animal kingdom. These are his favorite subjects; flowers and birds have the power of inspiring him with compositions which are charming in their truth, grace, and harmony. In regard to perfection of execution, the works produced in both capitals are equally admirable.

"Let us pause before a magazine of objects of art and industry, among the curious of both sexes and of all ages, who never cease to gather together under the covered gallery where the stores are displayed. They contemplate with a naïve admiration the great aquaria of blue or white porcelain, where red fish float in the limpid water over beds of shells. In the centre, three or four selected plants combine in a picturesque group the beauty of their colors and the graceful outlines of their leaves and flowers. Nothing of these combinations is ever left to chance: every day the gardener's hand directs the work of nature, keeps it within limits, and governs the growth.

"What is still more remarkable, the Japanese fancy never runs into those aberrations which in China and elsewhere, outrage Nature by cutting trees into geometrical figures, or training shrubs into the shapes of animals. The taste of the Japanese in their popular arts, remaining independent of the conventional influences of their two courts, has all the freshness of a naturally expanding civilization. Therefore, it is still characterized by a certain puerility: witness the truly childish passion of all classes of society for enormous flowers and dwarf trees. I have seen aquaria, not much larger than ordinary, where they succeeded in uniting the features of a complete landscape, — a lake, islands, rocks, a cabin on the shore, and hills with real woods on their summits, of living bamboos and cedars in miniature. They even sometimes add liliputian figures, coming and going, by means of a spring which is wound up.

"This sort of childishness is found in a multitude of the details of Japanese life. Sometimes a porcelain junk is set before a dinner party: it is taken to pieces and proves to be a unique and complete tea-set. Often, part of the repast is served in cups so minute, and porcelain so fine. light, and transparent, that one hardly dares to touch it. There are cups, called egg-shells, so delicate that they must be protected by a fine envelope of bamboo netting.

"The saloons are adorned with bird and butterfly cages, crowned with vases of flowers, whence depend climbing plants which cause the birds to appear as if nestling in verdure. Under the paper lanterns suspended from the ceilings of the verandas, there are often bells of colored glass, the long, slender clapper of metal supported by a silk thread, or slip of colored or gilded paper. At the least movement of the breeze these bands of paper move, the metallic tongues swing and touch the glass bells, and their vibrations make a vague melody, like the sound of an Æolian harp.

"I saw at Yedo some attempts at painting on glass, and some works in enamel, which exhibited good intentions rather than skill. I might mention, however, among the native curiosities which are truly original, those little balls of stone, pierced, cut in facets and covered with enameled arabesques, which strangers buy for necklaces. The art of gilding is still but partially developed. The narratives of the old Dutch embassies seem to have greatly exaggerated the richness of decoration of the palaces and furniture of the Mikado and the Tycoon. The luxury of the Japanese has an artistic rather than a sumptuous character. The pride of the old princes of the empire is in the antiquity of their arms or furniture. Nothing has more value in their eyes than an assorted service of old porcelain, naturally cracked, or vases of ancient bronze, heavy, black and polished as marble.

"Yedo is the city where metals are worked to the greatest extent. The bronze establishments of the city are among the most interesting curiosities of native art. Some present the appearance of great bazaars, displaying all articles of saddlery and harness, as well as complete suits of armor, and cooking utensils of iron, copper, or tin, beside the bronze objects. The latter contain many things belonging to Buddhist worship, such as richly-chased bells, drums, gongs, vases for the altar, crowns of lotus flowers, or vessels to hold bouquets of natural flowers. There are also altars for perfumes, resting on tripods, statues and statuettes of saints, and such sacred animals as the crane, stork, tortoise, and the fantastic Corean dog.

"Next to the master-pieces of bronze and of porcelain, the triumph of Japanese industry is in the fabrication of furniture and utensils of lacquered wood. Such is the talent with which the native artisans utilize the incomparable Japan varnish, the produce of the shrub which bears that name; such is their skill in combining its effects with the results of their decorative art, that articles of furniture constructed of a material which is almost valueless, finally rival in beauty, and almost in durability, those which we make of marble and precious metals. The ebony workers of Yedo imitate works in old lacquer so closely that only an experienced eye can detect the difference. In the interior decoration of cabinets, boxes, or caskets of modern taste, they generally used lacquer of a brown color, sprinkled with flakes of gold. On the outside the lacquer is uniform, either red, brown, or black, with ornamental drawing in two or three tints.

"The principal large objects made of lacquered wood are the *norimons* (palanquins) and travelling trunks of nobles, wardrobes, toilet tables, and the pedestals of mirrors for ladies; *etagères*, for costumes of ceremony, or for the books and scrolls of a library; and finally, different articles employed in public or private worship, such as pulpits, offering-tables, censer-stands, tripods for gongs, and pedestals for various purposes.

"Among the toilet articles there are several boxes, which vary in form and ornament according to their use, as for brushes, tooth-powder, rouge, rice-powder, and other cosmetics; for combs, hair-pins, and, alas! for false braids of hair. The other accessories of the feminine boudoir are, a large oval watering-pot, covered with black lacquer, sown with golden flowers; then a long box for pipes and tobacco, and finally a casket for letters, prudently bound by two silk cords, knotted in a way of which the owner alone knows the secret. There are other boxes of an oblong form, which are usually taken in Europe for gloves; but the Japanese only employ them in order to send letters of congratulation, or thanks, in a more polite way.

"The liquor *saki*, the serving of which is the most ceremonious part of a Japanese banquet, is solemnly brought to the guests in large lacquered pots, or long metal cans, on a bamboo tray. It is then heated in vessels of porcelain. The cups, large or small, are of fine red lacquer, ornamented with fancy designs. There are collections of these charming cups, each one of which represents a celebrated landscape of Japan, or one of the principal cities on the Tokaido connecting the two capitals. Some hosts, of a more sumptuous taste, invite the guests to drink from nautilus shells, mounted in silver filagree."

CHAPTER XVIII.

THE LITERATURE OF THE JAPANESE.

"THE higher schools which form the University of Yedo are perhaps the only neutral ground where the children of the Japanese nobility daily meet and live in common with those of the citizens. Nevertheless, the separation of rank exists between them in its usual severity. Their studies, also, differ in aim and character. The young gentlemen only receive a certain classical culture, based on the books of Chinese philosophers; while to scholars belonging to the *bourgeoisie* is opened the career of the liberal professions, such as the teaching of languages, the practice of medicine, or the places of interpreters, and civil engineers, under the government.

"The University of Yedo is not only placed under the patronage of Confucius; it also diffuses the doctrines of the Chinese philosopher, and establishes them among the lettered classes of Japanese society. This policy, however, is not exercised under the form of an aggressive propagandism, openly hostile to the established creeds; it spares the existing institutions, but destroys the faith which inspired them. I have heard an interpreter of Yedo say: 'The graduates of our University no longer believe anything,' and I know an official from the Castle, who, at a diplomatic dinner,

A JAPANESE SCHOOL.

graciously declared that respectable people in Japan, so far as religion is concerned, had reached the same level as the same class in other countries.

"The clergy, not feeling themselves menaced in their temporal position, maintain a modest and prudent attitude towards the literary class. The bonzes do not dare to attack the popularity with which the name of Confucius is surrounded, in Japan. He is universally venerated there, under the title of Koo-ci, a corruption of his Chinese name. But when one seeks to explain the influence which his writings have exercised on Japanese society, one must recognize that they have contributed, more than any other cause, not to the civilization, but to the *civility* which distinguishes it. The worship which is rendered to him, in the temple of the University at Yedo, as in China, is not properly an act of adoration, but a pious commemoration.

"It is true, nevertheless, that this homage degenerates into a superstitious respect for the text of the master, strengthened by the difficulties offered by the dry study of his works. For the study of a Chinese book is a labor the more arduous, even for the Japanese, because the language of the latter has no analogy with that of China. The Japanese tongue stands alone among the families of languages, and therefore is not only difficult to be learned, but also renders the acquirement of other languages difficult to those who speak it.

"Another source of confusion is the diversity of the Japanese dialects. At Hakodadi, there is one, quite distinct; another at Nagasaki, and a third in the Loo-Choo archipelago. In the island of Nipon is preserved the ancient idiom of Yamato, the classic language of Japan. The difficulties of the written language have only been overcome, as yet, by six or eight Europeans, missionaries, or members of the diplomatic corps. There are two distinct alphabets in use, the *Katakana*, which is used for the noble style and the impressions of sacred books, and the *Hirakana*, based upon the Chinese running-hand. Both are written from top to bottom, in columns beginning at the right hand of the page. The latter alphabet is used by the people, and for lighter literary works.

"The student of Yedo is obliged to prepare for a laborious career. Having acquired the *Hirakana* in his youth, he must also learn the *Katakana* in order to master the more serious productions of native literature, besides acquiring a sufficient knowledge of the Chinese language to read at least the works of Confucius and Mencius. Then he needs to make himself serviceable for public employment, or the liberal professions, by the most scrupulous observation of the laws of etiquette and society. The official style of the Japanese is sprinkled with particles and ceremonial phrases, which must never be omitted, or placed otherwise than according to the prescribed rules. Even the character of the manuscript differs, when an inferior addresses a superior, or the reverse.

"Miako was formerly the only cradle of literature in Japan. At present the old pontifical city preserves its specialty of albums for miniatures, almanacs of the Mikado, religious works, romances, and poems on velvet paper dusted with gold. But the presses of Yedo exceed in the number, the variety, the popularity, and the immense sale of their publications. The new literary works of the capital are due chiefly to Professors of the University or the advanced students of the College of Interpreters. Nearly all of them have a didactic character, a practical tendency, or some useful purpose. There is one which might be called a scientific annual, a review of inventions and discoveries, statistics of the countries of Europe and America, a manual of Modern History, another of Geography, and treatises on scientific, medical, naval, mechanical, and military subjects. The ancient Encyclopædias, which comprise more than two hundred volumes, are now replaced by a ' Lexicon of Conversation,' which appears annually in a single volume, illustrated with wood engravings. The chapters devoted to foreign nations are very destitute of critical appreciation : for instance, it is simply said of the Spaniards and Portuguese, that they have a very bad religion.

" As to the purely literary productions of the Japanese authors, we possess very little, and the selections made by the translators have not often been fortunate. More thorough research will doubtless lead to better results, but they will not be truly fruitful until after we have become familiar with the private life of the people, and the latter have furnished us with topics of their plays, legends, stories, and songs. They all have the passion of children for hearing the latter. As soon as the labors of the workmen and the currents of transportation have ceased, crowds of persons of both sexes may be seen, ranged in a semicircle around some professional declaimer, who squats upon some bench beside a wall. His recitations are given with considerable emphasis, but a limited use of mimicry. He interrupts them now and then, to drink a cup of tea or take a few whiffs from his pipe, the auditors, meanwhile, also smoking and exchanging remarks upon the theme of his story.

"Metrical romances and legendary songs are left to the women, who gain their bread as singers and musicians. They form a very numerous class; but only the inferior artists lead an entirely nomadic life. We generally meet them, very respectably dressed, under the verandas of the tea-houses, or in a sort of portable booth. In the more frequented gardens, there are pavilions which seem to be specially constructed for their use, often actual bowers of foliage and flowers, formed by the magnificent trees which abound in Japan, camelias and magnolias, paulownias and wisterias.

"The most distinguished singers only appear in company with three or four musicians, and do not themselves perform on any instrument. The orchestra which accompanies the pieces they offer, whether recitations or songs, consists of one or two samsins, or guitars, a species of violoncello, played with or without a bow, and a dulcimer with nine strings.

"One evening when we had attended a concert of musicians, I said to our yakounins, on the way home, that I regretted not being able to understand the words of their national ballads. They assured me, smiling and shrugging their shoulders, that I really lost nothing. One of them, nevertheless, politely added that collections of the songs and legends chanted at the teahouses could be obtained at the bookstores in the city.

I commissioned a courtier to buy me what he could find, and I had reason to believe that he faithfully executed my orders, for he brought me a whole library of stories, anecdotes, and ballads. Most of them being illustrated, it was not difficult for me to recognize the most popular subjects.

"They were principally heroic exploits, of the most astonishing and impossible character. But it would be difficult to give an idea of the more fantastic legends. The merit of the latter, which are expressed in very brief poems, seems to consist in the choice of expressions, in the structure of the verse, — in a word, in abstract elegance of style, for the translation very often gives something totally trivial, with no significance whatever.

"For example, what can be the point of the following? 'The soul of a very thievish weasel was hidden in the kettle of an old priest. The latter saw it issue therefrom, one day, when he had exposed the kettle to a hotter fire than usual.' This is all! and this stuff is the subject of one of the favorite pictures of the people.

"The worship of trees, which existed among all the people of antiquity, is rendered by the Japanese to those which are very old. When the lord of Yamato wished to make a complete set of furniture from the trunk of the oldest cedar of his park, the axe of the woodman bounded back from the bark, and drops of blood followed the blow. The legend says that ancient trees have souls, like men, on account of their great age. They also show themselves sensible of the misfortunes of the fugitives who seek their shelter. They have more than once saved behind the screen of their branches or in the cavernous hollow of their trunks, an unfortunate warrior, who would otherwise have fallen into the hands of his enemies.

"Animals, also, which attain a great age, finally receive souls like trees or human beings, and sometimes possess supernatural powers. The polecat, when it is old, summons from the tops of the mountains the wind and the clouds; hail and rain obey it. It rides forth on the wings of the hurricane. The traveller, surprised on his way, battles with the tempest, but his face is stung as if by the cut of a knife, from the claws of the polecat as it passes by. Old frogs, squatted around the edges of a pond, cause a thick mist to descend on the eyes of the belated countryman. The silver pheasant makes a mirror of his plumage, and is invulnerable to the arrows of the hunter. Old wolves have the power of metamorphosis. When travellers believe that they are pursuing their journey in safety, they meet in the evening, at the edge of a wood, a beautiful girl, carrying in her hand a lantern painted with bouquets of roses. But those who follow her are led directly into the jaws of a voracious wolf.

"In Japanese literature, there is a great number of moral tales, conceived in the same spirit as the 'Collection of Virtuous Actions,' of the school of Confucius. Their authors are generally men of letters, from the University of Yedo, school-masters, or writers employed by the booksellers, while the heroic and fantastic legends are the combined result of popular tradition and the imagination of the old bonzes who have remained faithful to the spirit of the national poetry. If some of the moral tales rival the popularity of the old legends, it is owing chiefly to the booksellers of Yedo, who either produce good and cheap editions of the former, or employ artists of talent and popularity to illustrate them.

"Our cosmopolitan age, so eager for new commercial outlets, will also acquire new sources of intellectual interest. Our European literature will lose nothing by issuing from its somewhat restricted horizon. Already the contemporary poetry of Germany has been enriched with many a jewel drawn from the inexhaustible stores of Persia and India; but the extreme Orient is still an untouched mine. From the little that has been given to the world, I take the following Japanese story, which is quoted by a Dutch author, Dekker, in his 'Max Havelaar':—

"'THE STONE-CUTTER.

"'Once upon a time there was in Japan a poor stone-cutter, a simple workman in the quarries. His life was rude, he worked much, gained little, and was not at all contented with his fate.

"'"O, if I could only be rich enough to rest, to sleep on thick matting, wrapped in a kirimon of soft silk!" Such was the sigh which he breathed to heaven. An angel intercepted it.

"'"It shall be according to thy desire," said the angel to him. And he at once became rich, and he rested, slept upon thick matting and wrapped himself in a kirimon of soft silk.

"'It happened that the Emperor passed by. He was preceded by heralds on foot and on horseback, followed by a brilliant escort of cavaliers, and surrounded by persons who held over his head an immense parasol resplendent with gold.

"'"What good does it do me to be rich?" murmured the man, "as long as I have not the right to go out with an escort, and my head protected by a golden parasol? Why am I not the Emperor?"

"'" Thou shalt be," said the angel.

"' And, indeed, he became the Emperor. He had an escort of cavaliers before and behind him, and people who held above his head an immense parasol resplendent with gold.

"' However, the sun, with his ardent beams, dried up the country, and the dusty road, quivering with his brightness, fatigued the eyes.

"'" It is a great advantage to be Emperor," cried the man, " when the heat of the day exhausts you, and the sun never ceases to make you feel his power! But if one could be the sun!"

"'" Behold! Are you satisfied?" the angel asked. For he had become the sun, and he darted his beams up and down, right and left, and all around him. And he scorched the herbage of the earth and the face of the princes upon the earth.

"' But now a cloud thrust itself between the earth and him; it held back the rays of the sun and prevented them from falling upon the earth's surface.

"'" There is strength," cried the sun, — " a cloud capable of resisting my power. It would be better if I were a cloud."

"'" Very well," said the angel.

"' And the transformation was at once accomplished. The new cloud placed itself haughtily between the sun and the earth, and so thoroughly intercepted the rays of the sun that it soon saw the earth covered with its shadow. Then it caused big drops of rain, and pouring showers and water-spouts to fall on the lands, so that the torrents burst their bounds and the rivers spread over and devastated the fields.

"'Nothing resisted the force of the inundation: only a rock defied it, perfectly motionless. In vain the bellowing waters beat it in their fury, the rock yielded not, but the foaming waves died at its foot.

"'"A rock, then, is my superior," said the cloud; "I would rather be in its place."

"'"You shall be," said the angel.

"'And he was transformed into a steep, unshaken rock, insensible to the rays of the sun, indifferent to the torrents of rain and the shock of the tumultuous waves.

"'Nevertheless, he distinguished at his feet a man of poor appearance, hardly clothed, but armed with a chisel and a hammer; and the man, with the help of these instruments, struck off pieces of the rock which he dressed into stones proper for cutting.

"'"What is that?" cried the rock: "has a man the power of rending pieces of stone from my breast? Shall I be weaker than he? Then it is absolutely necessary that I should be that man!"

"'"Have your will!" said the angel; and he became again what he had been, — a poor stone-cutter, a simple workman in the quarries. His life was rude, he worked much and gained little, but he was contented with his lot.'"

CHAPTER XIX.

RECREATIONS AND DOMESTIC CUSTOMS OF THE JAPANESE.

"THE races who possess the Chinese civilization have nothing similar to the beneficent Semitic institution of a day of rest, regularly recurring after a series of days of labor. They have monthly festivals, from which, however, the laboring classes derive but little benefit, and a whole week at the beginning of the year, during which all work is suspended, and the people of both city and country give themselves up to such recreations as they can afford.

"The citizens of Yedo, the artisans, the Japanese merchants and manufacturers, lived under economical conditions of the most exceptional character, until the arrival of Europeans. Only laboring for the internal consumption of a country highly favored by nature, sufficiently large and cultivated to supply all their needs, they enjoyed for centuries the charms of a life at once simple and easy. This state of things is passing away. I have seen the closing days of this age of innocence, in which, with the exception of some chief merchants, who seem to have been veritably pursued by a kindly fortune, people only worked enough to live, and only lived for the sake of enjoying life. Even labor might be classed in the category of enjoyments, for the workman grew enthusiastic over his work, and

COUNTRYMAN WINTER COSTUME.

instead of painfully counting the hours, days, and weeks devoted to it, he tore himself from it with reluctance when he had attained, not wealth, but a satisfactory degree of artistic skill. When surprised by fatigue, he was in the habit of resting at his ease, either alone in his own habitation, or in some place of public recreation in the company of his friends.

"There are few Japanese dwellings of the middle class which have not their little private gardens, quiet retreats for sleep, for reading, fishing in the tanks, or indulging in libations of tea and saki. The chains of hills which traverse the quarters to the south and west of the Castle are remarkably rich in rocks, little glens, grottoes, springs, and ponds, which the small proprietors combine in the most ingenious manner, so as to give the features of a varied landscape in a limited space. When there is an entrance from the garden upon the street, a rustic bridge is thrown over the canal before the portal, which is carefully concealed under spreading trees or thick shrubbery. We have hardly crossed the threshold, when we find ourselves apparently in a wild forest, far from all habitation. Masses of rocks, carelessly disposed in the manner of a staircase, invite us to ascend, and from the summit a charming view is suddenly spread out below. An amphitheatre of leaves and flowers incloses a picturesque pond of water, bordered with lotus, iris, and waterlilies; a light wooden bridge is thrown across it; the path which descends to the latter passes by long windings through clumps of bamboos, azaleas, dwarf palms, and camelias, then by groves of small pines and slopes of turf or flowers.

"In their fondness for harmonious effects, for quiet enjoyment and reverie bordering on abstraction, the Japanese show their tendency toward that condition of physical indifference and ideal annihilation which is inculcated by Buddhism. Yet they do not consciously practice it as a system, and many of their hygienic customs seem to conflict with it. Every Japanese, of whatever age, washes regularly in the morning, and takes a bath heated to a temperature of about 120° during the day. They remain from fifteen to thirty minutes in the water, sometimes immersed to the shoulders, sometimes only to the waist, taking the greatest care to prevent their heads from getting wet. It is therefore no wonder that congestion of the brain is frequent.

"A custom so universal soon acquires a conventional character, and thus the exposure of the bath is tacitly considered as something disconnected with public morals, like eating or sleeping. Each wealthy family, it is true, has its own bath-chamber, which is used either successively by the members of the household, or at the same time; but the greater part of the population use the public bathing establishments on account of their cheapness. The latter usually contain two large reservoirs, divided by a low partition, the women and children occupying one and the men the other; but it is also considered quite respectable to use them in common. It is also held to be proper for the bather to step into the street to cool himself, or even to walk home before dressing. It would be very unjust to judge this custom from the European point of view, and necessarily associate it with a low condition of morals among the Japanese.

CITIZEN OF YEDO. WINTER COSTUME.

"The kneading of the muscles of the body, as a cure for various maladies, is much practiced in Japan, but neither by the regular physicians nor those whose business is acupuncture or the application of the moxa. The kneaders are always chosen from among the blind, who form a grand brotherhood throughout the empire.

"It is very difficult for the stranger in Japan to share to any extent in the domestic life of the people, and hence almost impossible to witness their family festivals and ceremonies. In all the countries of the extreme East, the marriage of a girl is characterized only by the festivities which are held in the house of the bridegroom. But while the Chinaman is proud to invite foreign guests to the wedding of his daughter, in order to impress the former with the display, the Japanese, on the contrary, surrounds the ceremonies of the occasion with the most discreet reserve. He considers it too serious to be witnessed by any other than the nearest relations and friends of the two parties.

"Most of the Japanese marriages are the result of a family arrangement, prepared a long time in advance, and usually characterized by that practical good sense which is one of the national traits. The bride has no dowry, but she receives a very rich and complete *trousseau*. But it is necessary that she should have a spotless reputation, a gentle and amiable character, a proper education, and skill to conduct a household. Pecuniary considerations are of secondary importance, and they rarely take the form of money. When a father, who has no male child, gives his only or eldest daughter in marriage, her husband is called the adopted son of the family, takes the same name, and inherits the trade or business of his father-in-law.

"Marriage is preceded by a ceremony of betrothal, at which all the principal members of the two families are present. It often happens that the parties concerned then for the first time are informed of the intentions of their parents with regard to them. From this time, they are allowed every possible opportunity of seeing each other, and ascertaining the wisdom of the choice, wherein they were not consulted. Visits, invitations, presents, preparations for furnishing their future home, succeed each other, and the betrothed are soon satisfied with their approaching destiny.

"The wedding generally takes place when the bridegroom has attained his twentieth year, and the bride is in her sixteenth. Early in the morning of the appointed day the *trousseau* of the latter is carried to the bridegroom's house, and tastefully arranged in the rooms prepared for the festival. The images of the gods and the patron saints of the two families are also suspended there, before a domestic altar adorned with flowers and heaped with offerings. Lacquered tables support dwarf cedars and figures representing the Japanese Adam and Eve, accompanied by their venerable attributes, the centenary crane and tortoise. Finally, to complete the tableau by a lesson of morals and patriotism, there are always to be found among the presents a few packages of edible sea-weed, mussels, and dried fish, which suggest to the young couple the primitive nourishment and ancient simplicity of the Japanese people.

"Toward noon, a splendid procession enters the halls

JAPANESE MARRIAGE.

thus prepared: the young wife, clothed and veiled in white, advances, escorted by two bridesmaids and followed by a crowd of relations, neighbors, and friends, in festal costumes glittering with brocade, scarlet, gauze, and embroidery. The two bridesmaids perform the honors of the house, arrange the guests, order the courses of the collation, and flutter from one group to another to see that all are served. They are called the male and female butterfly, which insects they are expected to represent in the style and ornament of their garments.

"With the exception of certain Buddhist sects, which admit a nuptial benediction among their rites, a priest never takes part in the celebration of a Japanese marriage. There is nothing similar to a publication of the bans, but the police officer who has given permission for a nuptial festival in the quarter under his guardianship inscribes another couple upon his list. The public knowledge of the act, therefore, is as complete as possible.

"In place of our sacramental *Yes*, they have recourse to an expressive symbol. Among the objects displayed in the middle of the circle of guests, there is a metal vase, shaped like a basin, and furnished with two spouts. This utensil is elegantly adorned with bands of colored paper. At a certain signal, one of the ladies of honor fills it with saki; the other takes it by the handle, lifts it as high as the lips of the kneeling bride and bridegroom, and causes them to drink from it alternately, each from the spout on his or her side, until the liquor is exhausted. It is thus that, as husband and wife, they must together drain the cup of conjugal life, each drinking from one side, but both tasting the same ambrosia or the same wormwood.

"The poorer classes — one may say, the masses of the population — are generally free from the social vices which are encouraged among the higher classes by the license allowed to them. The households of the shopkeepers, artisans, laborers, and cultivators of the soil, exact the constant care and toil of the father and mother, the union of their efforts, in order to provide for the needs of their families. There are wedded couples who labor and save heroically for years, in order to pay the expenses of their marriage festival.

"There is one rather amusing custom, however, whereby this expense may be avoided. A couple of respectable people have a daughter, who is acquainted with a good young fellow who would be an excellent husband for her, except that he lacks the necessary means to give her the customary wedding-presents and keep a free table for a week, for the two families. The parents, coming home from the bath one fine evening, do not find their daughter at home. They inquire in the neighborhood; nobody has seen her, but all the neighbors offer their services in assisting to find her. The parents accept the offer, and the procession, constantly increasing in numbers, passes from street to street, until it reaches the dwelling of the lover. The latter, protected by his closed screens, in vain pretends to be deaf; he is at last obliged to yield to the demands of the crowd. He opens the door, and the lost daughter, in tears, throws herself at the feet of her parents, who threaten her with their malediction.

"Then, the tender-hearted neighbors, moved by the

scene, intercede; the mother relents; the father remains haughty and inexorable; the intercession of the neighbors increases in eloquence, and the young man promises to be the most faithful of sons-in-law. Finally, the resistance of the father is overcome; he pardons his daughter, pardons the lover, and calls the latter his son. All at once, as if by magic, cups of saki circulate among the crowd; every one takes his or her place on the matting of the room; the two outlaws are seated in the midst of the circle, drink their bowl of saki together, the marriage is proclaimed in the presence of a sufficient number of witnesses, and the police officer enters it upon his list the next morning.

"Bridal trips are unknown in Japan. Instead of leaving the newly-wedded pair to themselves, every pretext is employed to overwhelm them with visits and invitations, always accompanied with feasts and prolonged libations.

"On the thirtieth day after his birth every citizen of Nipon receives his surname, or rather his *first* name, for he has another at his majority, a third when he marries, a fourth if he assumes any public function, a fifth when he is promoted in rank, and so on until the last, which is given to him after his death and engraved upon his tomb, as the name by which he will be known to the succeeding generations. The ceremony which corresponds to our baptism is the simple presentation of the new-born child in the temple of his family deity. Except in certain sects, this act is not accompanied by the sprinkling of water or any form of purification. The father gives to the officiating bonze a note containing three names. The latter copies these upon three slips of paper, which he shuffles together, and then, loudly uttering a sacramental invocation, he casts them into the air, and the first slip which touches the floor of the sanctuary indicates the one of the three names which is most agreeable to the divinity. This the bonze writes at once on a sheet of holy paper, which he gives to the father as a talisman for the child.

"The baptism of a child is always an occasion of munificence on the part of the family towards the priests. The latter, of course, enter the child's name on their books, and never lose sight of it during all the changes of its after life. The registers of the monasteries have the reputation of being well kept, and they are always open to the examination of the officers of police. At the age of three, the boy begins to wear the girdle, and, if he is noble, at the age of seven the two swords indicative of his caste. The weapons, of course, are only provisional. First, when he is fifteen, he exchanges them for the hereditary weapons belonging to his family.

"Among the citizens, the three epochs are the occasion of festivals, which are only less important than that of marriage. On the very day when the boy is fifteen years old, he attains his majority, dresses his hair like a mature man, and takes part in the affairs of his paternal household. On the evening before, he is still addressed as a child; then, suddenly, the manner of those about him changes: the ceremonious forms of Japanese civility represent his emancipation to his own eyes; and he on his part, endeavors to respond to the congratulations of the others in such a manner as to show that he appreciates the responsibility of his new position. His testimony, in fact, is not confined to hollow assertions, and I do not hesitate to count among the most interesting traits of Japanese society, the care, the patience and seriousness with which boys of fifteen abandon the sports of childhood and devote themselves to the stronger discipline of practical life.

"Apprenticeship to a branch of manual labor implies a service of ten years. During this time the master furnishes food, lodging, and clothing, but no salary until towards the end of the term, when he gives the apprentice enough pocket money for his tobacco. He is interested in developing the latter's skill as much as possible, for he offers his name to the guild for membership, when he claims to be elected a master. The distinction cannot be conferred, however, until the workman is twenty-five years old. As soon as it has been obtained, he is free, and his former master furnishes him with all the utensils of his trade.

"In all Japanese families, death is the occasion of a series of domestic solemnities, more or less sumptuous, according to the rank of the deceased, but in every case a heavy expense to the nearest relatives. They must first pay the cost of the religious ceremonies which are performed by the bonzes; then the last sacraments; the watches and prayers which are kept up without interruption in the house of death until the funeral; the closing service before the procession departs; the funeral mass celebrated at the temple, and all the implements connected with the burning and inurning of the body, such as coffin, drapery, wax-candles, flowers, fuel, urn, tomb, and refreshments furnished to the priests. Finally the coolies who wash the body and carry the coffin have their turn, and then the laborers attached to the cemetery. This is not the end, for a pious custom imposes upon all who can afford it the duty of giving alms to all who come as beggars. Last of all when the procession returns, those who take part in it think themselves wanting in proper respect to the deceased, unless, before taking leave of the afflicted family, they sit down to a banquet prepared for them.

"The head of the corpse is always shaved and the body carefully washed in warm water in the bath-room. When the attendants have finished their work, they lift it up in order to introduce it into the coffin, which is not always easy. The rich Japanese, who prefer inhumation, are put into large jars, made for the purpose by the native potters. It is said that a good deal of energy is necessary, and sometimes an application of blows in order to force the body, and especially the shoulders, into these narrow receptacles. The poorer people use, instead, a single cask of pine staves, with bamboo hoops.

"The funerals of the poor are attended by a very small number of relatives and friends, who, in confusion and with hurried pace, endeavor to reach by sunset the gloomy valley where bodies are burned under the charge of some inferior priest from a neighboring monastery. The pariahs of Japanese society, who are outside the pale of religious aid, disdain all ceremony. They simply carry the dead bodies of their brethren to some deserted spot, where they collect wood and, lighting the fire with their own hands, reduce the remains to ashes.

"Finally, still lower than this class — that is, lower than those artisans who ply unclean trades, such as skinners, tanners, and curriers, lower than executioners, lepers, cripples, and beggars — there is in Japan a class of individuals branded with the basest degree of legal infamy. They are the *christans*, — the descendants of the families of native Christians, which were not entirely destroyed in the persecutions of the seventeenth century. Their condition, in fact, is worse than that of the pariahs, who, among themselves, enjoy a species of liberty. The law ignores them so completely that the ground occupied by their camps of straw huts, is not counted in measuring distances along the roads. The *christans*, on the contrary, are assembled within the cities, in a quarter like the Jewish Ghetto of the Middle Ages, or even a sort of prison, when there are few of them. The police watch them from birth to death, taking care to make away with their corpses, no one knows how nor whither, but in such a way that the name of the Crucified shall not be pronounced over them.

"In a word the respect for the dead, or the sepulchral worship, which is apparently one of the estimable features of the Buddhist religion, only exists among the privileged classes, and in proportion as the bonzes draw a profit from it. The mode of burial, the form of the coffins, and above all the practice of burning, introduced by the priest Toseo in the year 700, allow the monasteries to divide and subdivide the lots of ground belonging to them. A small inclosure suffices for a family, for a number of generations."

CHAPTER XX.

SOJOURN IN THE HARBOR.

" AN ingenious machination of the Tycoon's **Governors** of Foreign Affairs shortened our first residence in Yedo, in a manner which was not very courteous. The government had already bound itself, in writing, to conclude a treaty with Switzerland; but when I asked for the fulfillment of the promise, the Japanese ministers urged that imperious circumstances obliged them to postpone it. At this period, it is true, the political consequences of the establishment of foreigners in Japan excited the growing hostility of the feudal dynasties. The Mikado, under the pressure of this hostility, had refused to sanction the treaties to which the Tycoon had subscribed. At Miako, the proposition was made to close the port of Yokohama, and effect the expulsion of the Europeans from all parts of Nipon.

"In this emergency, the Tycoon's counsellors endeavored to give the foreign legations the most tranquilizing assurances of the maintenance of their relations, and at the same time to satisfy the Court of the Mikado as far as possible without coming to a rupture with the Western Powers. Thus, by a skillful system of small daily annoyances, they drove the foreign consulates from the suburb of Kanagawa, where they had estab-

THE MIKADO OF JAPAN.

lished themselves, in accordance with the treaties. It was then decided to apply the same discipline to the legations at Yedo. When, finally, there only remained the Legation of the United States, devastated by fire, and the embassy of the Swiss Republic, the agents of the Castle supposed that the remainder of their task could be accomplished at one blow.

"One evening, on returning from a walk, a Governor of Foreign Affairs appeared suddenly, and mysteriously asked to speak to me without witnesses. He informed me that the party hostile to the Tycoon was in the ascendency; all the great daimios had withdrawn to Miako, and the Tycoon himself was obliged to hasten thither. If we should remain in Yedo during his absence, we should be menaced by great dangers, for the princes had left bravos behind them, conspired to destroy every vestige of a foreign legation. The American Minister, he said, was to embark that very night on a Japanese steamer for Yokohama.

"I replied that I would not leave without a letter from the government, stating the circumstances which compelled it to remove me from the capital. At the same time I dispatched a messenger, who brought me news that the members of the American Legation had embarked. I then determined to join them and ascertain the cause of their sudden departure.

"It was already night when we took the boat; our yakounins had theirs, and followed us at a short distance. The sky was overcast, and flocks of crows circled over our heads, on their way to the shore. After an hour and a half of navigation, we found a large steamer oeyond the detached forts. The American Minister met me at the top of the gangway, and we exchanged a few hasty words while the anchors were lifted. Suddenly the wheels began to move, and my companions and myself had only time to jump into our boat and get clear of the steamer. The chief of the escort then announced to me that he had orders not to allow us to return to the city at such an hour, at the same time indicating a vessel where we could pass the night.

"This vessel was none other than the Imperial yacht, the famous *Emperor*, presented to the Tycoon by Lord Elgin, in the name of Queen Victoria, ' with as much propriety,' says Mr. Oliphant, ' as if we should present a wife to the Pope.' It seemed to us, nevertheless, that the beautiful vessel well fulfilled its destiny, in harboring the Swiss Legation. The commander received us amicably, and opened two virgin cabins, that of the Tycoon, with divans enough to make four beds, and the other arranged for the use of the Tycooness, with every little detail of furniture which a lady could desire. But the next morning I could better appreciate the contrasts offered by our floating habitation: on one side the mirrors, gilding, silk and velvet of the Imperial cabins, on the other, a mixture of lazzaroni and yakounins encamped on the deck, sleeping, smoking, drinking tea, grinding rice, or playing games with their fans.

"I asked the yakounins to take me back to the Tjoodji. They called the boats, at once, and also agreed to make an excursion on horseback through the northern suburbs, during the day. I, however, remained at home, where I soon received the visit of a delegation from the Castle. I was informed that my demand gave great embarrassment to the government; nevertheless, I persisted in repeating it. Towards evening, one of the governors brought me word that the request had been granted, but I was expected to pass another night in the harbor.

"The evening was stormy, with a rough sea. There were two boats, the first occupied exclusively by our Japanese escort. We noticed that it was not making for the yacht, but for a large war steamer, on the deck of which there were suspicious movements. The stack was not smoking, yet it would be easy to fire up and hoist the anchor during the night. We therefore directed our own boat towards the Imperial yacht, disregarding the cries of the officials, who ordered us to follow them. On reaching the yacht, we found the ladder lifted, and the vessel silent and dark from one end to the other. The younger members of our party climbed to the deck and lowered the ladder; when we were all on board, the commander appeared. I explained to him that our escort had gone wrong, since we had agreed with the officials to return to his vessel for the second night. He at once had the cabins opened, and brought us lamps and saki. We thus remained in peaceable possession of the yacht, the first and only maritime conquest ever made by Switzerland!

"We remained six nights on board. The government accepted the arrangements which I proposed, and provided with dignity for our formal departure. Since they were no longer embarrassed by the protection of the Legation, and considered us rather as hosts, they allowed us liberty to dispose of our days, only insisting that we should not remain in the city after sunset. Except an attempt to detain some of the party at the landing-place, nothing occurred to disturb our final excursions; everywhere, in the most frequented streets, as within the precincts of the most popular temples, we met with the same reception, at the same time friendly and curious.

"Our maritime residence gave us the opportunity of getting acquainted with the fishers of the bay, who constitute, with the exception of the pariahs, the lowest class of the population. They live in the southern suburbs of the city and the Hondjo. When the tide is low, many rocks and piles around the five forts are uncovered, and the boats which take occasion of the ebb to go out on the bay, leave some of their crews on these dry spots, — especially young men, with all the implements necessary for fishing. There, standing or squatting, with a burning sun above their heads, and the dazzling mirror of the sea at their feet, they stand as motionless as so many cranes or herons. If we watch them steadily, we see them, from time to time, draw out a fish by the hook. They put the prize into a long bag of network, fastened to their waists, and hanging in the water, so that the captured fish are preserved alive and fresh.

"The bay of Yedo is almost as lively by night as by day, for the boats of the fishermen also go forth to engage in fire-fishing. Each bark bears at its prow a species of grating wherein they burn reeds and tar. Sometimes they form an immense semicircle, which

FÊTE OF THE SEA-GOD.

produces at a distance the effect of a quay sparkling with thousands of lamps.

"These tribes of the fishers of Yedo, this population so destitute of the goods which attach men to the soil, have all the stronger affection for the element which nourishes them. The seaman knows no finer festivals than those which are celebrated beside or in the sea. When the shore-dwellers of Sinagawa celebrate the anniversary of their divinity, Tengou, the winged god, the grotesque and jovial messenger of heaven, they can imagine no better way of demonstrating their respect for him than by carrying him into the sea. While the veterans of the monastery and their domestics are engaged in the annual purification of the temple and its furniture, the most vigorous priests hoist upon their shoulders the litter on which rests the throne of their divine patron, and, on reaching the strand, they take off their sacerdotal garments, and breast the waves in good order. The crowds of fishermen who tumultuously follow them soon surround the procession; seizing with their strong arms the holy shrine of the idol, they lift it above the lacquered hats of the bonzes, and notwithstanding the real or simulated efforts of its official guardians, who struggle with the crowd in the midst of the waves, the throne accomplishes its maritime pilgrimage, tottering, but still upright, in the hands of the people. This celebration is called the *matsouri* of Gots-Tennoo. It takes place on the sixth day of the sixth month (July or August), and is continued, with different rites, until the eighth day, when the bonzes, in conclusion, distribute among their flock branches laden with fruits half ripe, as the people prefer them.

"It is a curious fact, and one which seems inconsistent with the affection of the Japanese for the sea, and their habits of bathing, that they never take sea-baths. It cannot be the fear of imaginary monsters, for they are ready enough to enter the water during these religious processions."

NEW YEAR'S FESTIVITIES.

PROCESSION OF THE WHITE ELEPHANT.

CHAPTER XXI.

JAPANESE FESTIVALS AND THEATRES.

"THE religious festivals of the temples in Japan render to the government of the country a service which would be highly appreciated in Europe: they relieve it of the trouble of amusing its subjects. The latter, moreover, supply from their own means whatever they may find wanting. There are five grand annual festivals, the religious character of which does not in any wise detract from the gayety of the manifestations, for the old Kami creed declares that a joyous heart is always pure.

"The festival of the first day of the first month is naturally one of the most important. It is that of congratulations and presents, which at least consist in two or three fans which the visitor brings in a lacquered box, bound with cords of silk. Nevertheless, whatever be the nature or the value of the present, it must always be accompanied by a paper cone containing a piece of dried fish of the commonest sort, as a souvenir of the frugality of the ancestors. The family which receives the visit furnishes refreshments, consisting of saki, rice cakes, and mandarin oranges.

"The second, called the Festival of the Dolls, takes place on the third day of the third month. It is devoted to the female children. The mothers adorn the chamber of state with blossoming peach-boughs, and arrange therein an exhibition of all the dolls which their daughters have received. They are pretty figures, handsomely costumed, and representing the Mikado, and other personages of the Imperial Court. A complete banquet is prepared for them, by the hands of the children when they are old enough, and the friends of the family help to consume it in the evening.

"The fifth day of the fifth month is the Festival of tne Banners, celebrated in honor of the boys. Let the reader imagine a great city like Yedo, planted with bamboo staffs, surmounted with plumes or balls of gilded paper and supporting long paper pennons of every color, floating in the wind; others with fishes of woven straw or varnished paper, but the greater part with lofty banners blazoned with coats-of-arms, family names, patriotic sentences, or heroic figures. It is a charming spectacle, especially when seen from a gallery overlooking one of the principal streets. Crowds of young boys in gala dresses circulate through the public ways, some having two little sabres like those of the yakounins in their belts, others bearing on their shoulders enormous swords of wood, painted in various colors and tied with paper ribbons, and still others carrying miniature banners.

"The Feast of Lanterns is the fourth, and occurs on the seventh day of the seventh month. At Yedo, the little girls go in crowds through the illuminated streets of the city, and sing with all their might while swinging with the right hand a paper lantern as large as they can manage. In some of the southern cities, the people visit the sepulchral hills, and pass the night among the tombs.

JAPANESE FESTIVAL OF THE BANNERS

"The fifth festival takes place on the ninth day of the ninth month, and is called the Feast of Chrysanthemums. At all the family repasts during the day, the leaves of chrysanthemum flowers are scattered over the cups of tea and saki. It is believed that the libations prepared in this manner have the power of prolonging life. The citizen of Yedo would consider that he was wanting in his duty as a good husband and father if he should partake sparingly of this specific.

"Masquerades are also very common, and one sees many varieties of dancing. The 'rice dance' alone contains thirty different figures; it is performed only by men whose costume is a girdle of rice straw, a round hat of the same, and a little floating mantle, the broad sleeves of which resemble the wings of a moth.

"The other festivals, and the religious or symbolical processions, occur very frequently, and present the greatest diversity in their character. There is the festival of the Lion of Corea, of the Foxes, of the patron of the sacred dances, and many others. The procession of the White Elephant has an enormous pasteboard representation of the animal, marching on the feet of men inclosed in each one of the four legs. He is preceded by Tartar music, wherein the sound of flutes and trumpets is mixed with the noise of drums, cymbals, gongs, and tambourines. The men who take part in this festival wear beards, pointed hats, boots, a long robe bound by a girdle, and some of them carry waving banners covered with figures of dragons.

"In order to shorten the time which intervenes between the festivals, the good people of Yedo have made for themselves a thousand other resources for amusement and recreation. There are both temporary and permanent occasions; by night and by day; on the highways, in the temples and their precincts, in special buildings, circuses, or theatres. The means of all classes are consulted; even the *Sibaïa*, which corresponds to our Grand Opera, is accessible to the common people, yet it has never received or solicited the least subsidy from the city or national government.

"The character of the popular diversions varies according to the quarter of the city, as in other great capitals. The aristocracy have their race-courses, their pugilistic exhibitions, and their classic drama, the citizens their genteel comedy, and the common people their jugglers and mountebanks, while there are permanent fairs where all these forms of amusement may be enjoyed at any time. There are circuses, where the riders perform the usual feats upon trained horses, but they are stationary, like the theatres.

"The fair-ground of Yamasta may be called the Champs Elysées of Yedo. Porters sprinkle with water the macadamized avenues; the double rows of trees protect with their shade the troops of merry children, some running after a showman with a dancing monkey, others crowding around the sellers of jumping-jacks and artificial butterflies. On the broad sidewalks, shaded with maple-trees, which run parallel with the principal highway, little dealers, squatted in rows, each on his straw mat, exalt their several wares. It is a picturesque collection of signs with colored figures and great Chinese characters. The merchant who sells death to rats has an assortment of his victims around him, their swollen corpses demonstrating the powerful

effects of the drug to the spectators. His neighbor exhibits the head and paws of a bear to prove that it is genuine bear's-grease which he sells. Then come the mysterious little books of a fortune-teller: a little horned imp answers the conjurer's questions by striking a plate with a hammer.

"The nearer we approach the great square of Yamasta, the more the crowd increases. The sidewalks are invaded by portable booths, made of bamboo and matting. Here and there, nevertheless, some bolder adventurers succeed in keeping the public at a distance. Such, for instance, are the popular astronomer, and the dealer in the latest news. The first exhibits the best planetary system to a circle of auditors, and adds to the charm of his demonstration the mysterious attraction of a long opera-glass, by means of which each one may satisfy himself in regard to the sun, moon, and stars. The second, an old fellow with a nasal voice, mechanically repeats the history of the last execution, and distributes leaf by leaf, to the passers who offer him money, the printed sheets which he carries over his left arm. Sometimes these productions of the Yedo press add to the city news a brief account, illustrated with wood-cuts, of recent events throughout the world.

"Although there are no politics as yet, even the national history not yet having been compiled from the collections of annals, these printed sheets nevertheless contain the germ of publicity and political discussion. I made a collection of pamphlets which treated of the American war, of President Lincoln, of the fight between the *Monitor* and the *Merrimac;* and such publications must in time give a kind of political education to the Japanese people. Who can say, in fact, that the change has not already commenced? In the theatres of Yedo the new pieces frequently have a vein of political or religious satire more or less concealed; even the costumes of the ancient Mikados are introduced into burlesque dances.

"The fair-ground of Yamasta contains from twenty to thirty exhibitions of jugglers, mountebanks, reciters of legends, domestic comedies or historic masquerades. There are also two circuses, and at the entrances of the public gardens, or along the four sides of the open space, a multitude of little restaurants, booths for singing and dancing, and other similar diversions. The constructions are all of bamboo, boards, matting, and prepared paper; yet there is such a luxury of signs, such a display of brilliant colors, so many banners and pictures, that the general effect is in the highest degree gay and attractive.

"The grand theatre of Japan, the *Sibaïa*, has no historic character; the only court theatre is that of the Mikado. The residents of the Castle in Yedo affect to despise scenic representations. The theatre, therefore, offers a favorable field for the encouragement of native dramatic literature; but the authors unfortunately, have not yet succeeded in emancipating themselves from the Chinese school and its conventional dramatic characters.

"The Sibaïa, nevertheless, is one of the most interesting curiosities. In China, the public witnesses the performance and criticises the actors; in Japan, the public takes part in the piece in concert with the actors, exchanges sentiments with them, and thus acts also, as in some of the popular Italian theatres. The dramatic authors, who write for these theatres, reside in Yedo, where the plays are first produced, then repeated in the provinces afterwards The comedians of the capital have their annual holiday season, during which they perform in other cities. They are composed exclusively of men; women appear only in grand ballets, never as actresses.

"The announcement of the performance always takes before sunset. A delegation of actors in ordinary costume appears on platforms before the entrance; there, fan in hand, they address the crowd, explain the subject of the play, and describe the merits of the principal performers. Then follow jokes, witticisms, merry remarks by the crowd, mimicry, and a display of the great art of managing the fan. The lanterns are lighted, and the whole theatre becomes gradually illuminated, while the spectators enter and take their seats. There is always a restaurant, decorated with equal brilliancy, attached to each theatre.

"The interior is of an oblong form, with two tiers of boxes, the upper one containing the best seats. Here there are many ladies in full toilette, that is, muffled up to the eyes in crapes and silks; in the lower tier there are only gentlemen. The parterre resembles a chess-board. It is divided into compartments, each containing from eight to twelve seats, most of which are rented by the year to families who always take their children with them, and sometimes their visitors from the country. There are no passages, but all must find their places by walking along the tops of the divisions between the compartments. Tobacco and refreshments are served during the evening in the same manner.

"The drop-curtain always bears a gigantic inscription in Chinese characters. While waiting for it to rise, the spectators frequently become impatient, and sometimes an altercation takes place in the compartment assigned to the coolies, next to the stage. Then the actors take part in the debate, creeping forth under the curtain, or thrusting their heads through holes in it. When order is reëstablished some of the coolies climb upon the stage, and assist in rolling up the curtain.

"The performance usually lasts until one o'clock in the morning. It consists of a comedy, a tragedy, an opera with ballet, and two or three interludes of jugglers and gymnasts. The appearance of infernal characters is always preceded by a flash of lightning. The celebrated actors are accompanied by two domestics, who carry bamboo sticks with candles at the end, by which they illuminate the best poses, gestures, and expressions of face, so that the spectators shall lose nothing. The same thing occurs in the ballets.

"In the theatre of Gankiro, the dances are performed by young girls from seven to thirteen years of age. They also produce little operas, fairy extravaganzas, and ballets with the most fantastic costumes, such as birds and butterflies. These performances are characterized both by ingenuity and elegance, and many of them would compare favorably with similar pieces on the European stage.

"The jugglers and mountebanks are also distinguished by the variety and originality of their feats For instance, they perform a series of tricks by means

JAPANESE THEATRE.—SCENES BEHIND THE CURTAIN

JAPANESE FESTIVALS AND THEATRES. 207

of an enormously long false nose. One will lie down upon his back, with a boy balanced on the end of the nose, the boy supporting an open umbrella on the end of his own nose. Another will hold up his foot, upon the sole of which a boy plants his nose, and balances himself in the air. Some of these feats seem impossible, without the aid of some concealed machinery.

"I was witness to some astonishing specimens of illusion. After a variety of tricks with tops, cups of water, and paper butterflies, the juggler exhibited to the spectator a large open fan which he held in his right hand, then threw into the air, caught by the handle in his left hand, squatted down, fanned himself, and then, turning his head in profile, gave a long sigh, during which the image of a galloping horse issued from his mouth. Still fanning himself, he shook from his right sleeve an army of little men, who presently, bowing and dancing, vanished from sight. Then he bowed, closed the fan and held it in his two hands, during which time his own head disappeared, then became visible, but of colossal size, and finally reappeared in its natural dimensions, but multiplied four or five times. They set a jar before him, and in a short time he issued from the neck, rose slowly into the air, and vanished in clouds along the ceiling.

"At the fair of Asaksa, in addition to the performances of jugglers of all kinds, there are collections of animals which have been taught to perform tricks — bears of Yeso, spaniels which are valuable in proportion to their ugliness, educated monkeys and goats. Birds and fish are also displayed in great quantities. But the most astonishing patience is manifested by an old Corean boatman, who has trained a dozen tortoises, large and small, employing no other means to direct them than his songs and a small metal drum. They march in line, execute various evolutions, and conclude by climbing upon a low table, the larger ones forming, of their own accord, a bridge for the smaller, to whom the feat would otherwise be impossible. When they have all mounted, they dispose themselves in **three or four piles like so many plates.**"

TORTOISE CHARMER.

CHAPTER XXII.

VARIETIES OF JAPANESE LIFE.

THE Japanese are of medium stature, physically inferior to the Germanic races, but with some little resemblance to the inhabitants of the southern part of Portugal. There is a greater difference in the proportion between the height of the sexes than is found in Europe. According to the observations of Dr. Mohnike, formerly physician to the Dutch factory at Desima, the medium height of the men is five feet, two inches, and that of the women four feet, three inches. In the neighborhood of Yedo, however, men of six feet are not unusual.

The Japanese, without being precisely disproportioned, have generally large heads, slightly set within the shoulders, broad breasts, long bodies, and short legs. Their feet and hands are small, and often very beautiful. The form of the cranium has much more resemblance to the Turanian than the Mongolian races. The hair is invariably soft, thick, and as black as ebony. The men have a full beard, which they shave every alternate day. The color of the skin varies, according to the different classes of society, between the dark, copper tint of the natives of Java and the pale, golden olive of the South of Europe. The peculiar yellow complexion of the Chinese is never seen among them. Their children have rosy cheeks, and all the other signs of health and growth, as with the European races.

The Japanese women are fairer than the men. Many of those belonging to the higher classes of society are perfectly white, and a uniform pallor of complexion is esteemed by them as a sign of aristocratic blood. Nevertheless, they have two features which will always distinguish them from the pure Caucasian type, — the oblique eye, and an ungraceful depression of the bosom, which is found even in the youngest and most beautiful. Their teeth are almost always white, sound, and regular, and the practice which prevails among the married women, of staining them black, is as hideous as it is unnatural.

The mobility of expression, of which the Japanese countenance is capable, together with the great variety of physiognomy they exhibit, are the results of a more active, free, and original intellectual development than any other Asiatic race exhibits at present. This circumstance explains their remarkable capacity for adapting themselves to all the conditions of modern civilization.

In their houses, the matting of rice-straw, which is four inches thick, renders all other furniture nearly unnecessary. It is the mattress on which the Japanese sleeps, enveloped in an ample gown and a wadded quilt, with his head upon a little wooden pillow; it is the table-cloth whereon he sets the lacquered dishes which contain his repast; it is a carpet for the bare feet of his children, and a divan where, squatted on his heels, he invites his friends to squat in like manner and give themselves up to interminable gossip, with the never-failing accompaniments of tea and tobacco.

"One day," says M. Humbert, " when I was present at the recitations of half a dozen small boys, seated around their school-master, I inquired the meaning of the words which they repeated in chorus. I was told that they were learning to recite the *Irova*, a sort of alphabet in which the Japanese have united and arranged in four lines, not the vowels and consonants, but the fundamental sounds of their language. The number of these is fixed at forty-eight, and in place of classifying them as elements of language according to their relation to the organs of speech, they are thrown together as a little poem, the first word of which, *Irova*, gives its name to the alphabet. I quote it exactly, with the preliminary explanation, that the consonant *v* is sometimes pronounced like *f* and sometimes like an aspirated *h*, in certain Japanese dialects ; that the *w* is always pronounced as in English ; and that the sounds of *d* and *t* are frequently confounded, as well as those of *g* and *k*, *s* and *ds*, *z* and *ts*. I should therefore not be surprised if a Japanese alphabet were still to be constructed for the use of Europeans. However that may be, this is the verse : —

> "Irova nivovéto tsirinourou wo,
> Wagayo darézo tsouné naramon.
> Ou wi no okouyama kéfou koyéte,
> Asaki youmémisi évimo sézou oun."

"That which particularly interested me, indeed, impressed me very profoundly, is the signification of this quatrain which is recited daily, throughout the Empire, by so many millions of little human beings, who are immortal souls, no less than we : —

> "Color and perfume disappear.
> In our world, what can be permanent?
> The present day has vanished in the abyss of nothingness.
> It was the frail form of a dream: it disturbs us not."

"Verily this national alphabet reveals more of the inherent character of the Japanese people than many large volumes. For ages past, the generations which go repeat to the generations which come: 'There is nothing permanent in this world; the present passes like a dream, and its flight disturbs us not in the least.' The peculiar manifestations of the religious sentiment in Japan give evidence that this popular philosophy of annihilation does not satisfy the needs of the soul; but it acts, nevertheless, as a constant force, the results of which are manifest in many details of life.

"For example, this feeling undoubtedly contributes to the suppression of domestic comforts, of that family sentiment which has its own traditions and inherited habits. All that is poetic in the lives of the Japanese comes from their harmony with the external world. When night comes, the screens of the dwellings are closed, the chambers are put in order for sleeping, and a single lamp is lighted in a lofty wooden frame, covered with oiled paper, giving hardly more light than that of the stars. But with morning, all the furniture belonging to slumber is taken away and put into a closet. The screens are opened on all sides, and the dwelling is swept from one end to the other. The air circulates everywhere, and the sunshine falls in broad bars across the matting. Then, during the hot hours of the day, the house is again so thoroughly closed that it seems like a gloomy cavern, and becomes the abode of the most absolute indolence and repose.

" The children draw the most profit from this manner of living without any lively remembrance of the past, any particular care for the future. The Japanese fathers and mothers recognize that childhood has its own laws, and therefore, without much concerning themselves about discipline, they find in their children, from day to day, a source of amusement and recreation. Those travellers who declare that the Japanese children never cry have only exaggerated an actual circumstance.

" The Japanese is the husband of a single wife, who enters upon her household duties at so early an age, that, in every respect save the happiness of her children, it is a positive evil. She passes almost without transition from playing with a doll to playing with a child, and she retains her own childish character for a long while. On the other hand, the national custom does not permit her to raise her children effeminately. The baby must be hardened to atmospheric influences by exposing it every day to the air, and even to the midday sun, completely naked and with its head shaved. In order to carry it with the least fatigue, she sets it upon her shoulders between the chemise and the collar of her *kirimon*. In the dwellings, the children may safely be left to themselves, to tumble upon the matting as they please, for there is no furniture against which they might injure themselves.

" For playmates they have domestic animals, — a sort of little rabbit with short legs and a plump, fat body, and a distinct breed of cats, with white fur marked with yellow and black spots, bad mousers, indolent, but affectionate animals. Like those of Java, they have no tails. There is no family in tolerable circumstances which does not possess an aquarium containing many varieties of fish, red, silver, golden, round as a ball, or with large palmated fins, thin and transparent as gauze. They have also cages of bamboo, constructed after the model of the most elegant houses, where, upon beds of flowers, may be seen clusters of brilliant butterflies, or large katydids, the piercing, monotonous note of which is very agreeable to the natives.

"This is an outline, at least, of the surroundings amid which the Japanese child grows and is freely developed. In the first place he has all the influences of nature and the open air, then the paternal dwelling, which is hardly more than a sheltered gallery. His parents stint him neither in playthings, plays, nor festivals, as much on account of their own amusement as in the interest of his education. His lessons consist in little else than chanting the *Irova* and other exercises in reading, and in drawing with a pencil and India ink the letters of the alphabet, then words, and finally phrases. His emulation is not excited, and he is not hurried in his instruction, because the latter is a matter of general utility, and can only be slowly acquired. The idea of withholding his children from being taught never occurs to any parent. There is no educational system in the country, and no compulsory law; yet the entire adult population of both sexes is able to read, write, and calculate."

JAPANESE WRESTLERS.

CHAPTER XXIII.

THE GYMNASTS AND WRESTLERS.

THE Japanese have an equal passion for gymnastic sports and feats of strength, as for dramatic representations. For many centuries they have had a regular class of trained performers, who often attain a remarkable degree of skill. One of the first entertainments they offered to Commodore Perry, after the treaty of Yokohama, was a wrestling match between some of their famous champions of the ring; and they still delight in having foreigners witness displays of strength and agility, which, they imagine, are not equaled anywhere else in the world.

M. Humbert gives the following description of the performances of this class, both in the streets and booths. "In the public squares, the shouts and the sound of tambourines of two troops of gymnastic mountebanks, installed at opposite corners, are heard above the voices, songs, and clatter of implements of labor in the surrounding work-shops. One of these troops performs in the open air, its heroes being the swallower of swords, and the prodigious jumper. The latter leaps with impunity through two hoops crossed at right angles, fixed on the top of a pole, which also supports a jar carefully balanced on the intersecting hoops. But his most remarkable feat consists in leaping, or rather flying, from end to end through a cylinder of bamboo latticeworks, six feet long, and placed on trestles. When he wishes to excite the amazement of the spectators to the highest pitch, the performer lights four candles and places them in a line, at regular intervals, in the interior of the cylinder; after which he passes through like a flash, without extinguishing or deranging them.

" His gentle spouse, seated on a box beside the cylinder, accompanies the different stages of the performance with airs on her guitar. To the shrill sounds of the instrument she adds, from time to time, the tones of a voice which is either hoarse and hollow, or piercingly elevated, according as she judges it better to encourage sternly or to celebrate triumphantly the prowess of the astonishing man whose fortunes she is permitted to share.

" The other troop is that of the gymnasts of Miako. They perform in a vast shed, filled with such apparatus as masts, bars, and parallels, differing little from those of our gymnasia. The ever-useful bamboo furnishes all the necessary material. The troop is numerous, certain of their feats, trained to all enterprises of daring, and all the finer graces of their profession. They have no regular clown; each one is his own buffoon, and knows how to pass in an instant, with the most perfect ease, from the comical to the sublime, or the reverse. The most original part of the representation, to the European eyes, is the simplicity of the gymnastic costume. They have no idea of the *tricot*, or flesh-colored " tights," and their wardrobe consists only of two pocket-handkerchiefs tied around the loins. Their head-dress is a burlesque imitation of the bonnets of the princes or the mitre of the Mikado. They do not lay it aside, either when they perform on the bars and masts, or even when they perform the difficult feat of picking up by two toes a straw bee-hive lying on the ground, and placing it upon the head with the foot alone, while standing motionless with folded arms.

"The people of Yedo seemed to me to be only moderately interested in these gymnastic representations. They are not sufficiently dramatic for their taste. They prefer the emotions excited by the spectacle of man struggling with man, or with the laws of the material world. They insist that even their theatrical performances should overcome stubborn obstacles, and encounter serious dangers, for their pleasure. Above all, they require that new aliment shall constantly be furnished, to gratify their appetite for what is fantastic and marvelous. It is not enough that the rope-dancers perform the most remarkable feats of equilibrium with grace and agility: the rope must be stretched at a great elevation, and the dancer must undergo the most sudden and violent jerks, while balancing himself on one foot, in such a manner that his fall appears inevitable to the spectators.

"Neither is it enough for the people that the jugglers are as skillful with the left hand as with the right; they must train their toes to an equal dexterity. Even the wrestling-match, which, with the Greeks, and even now with the Swiss mountaineers, was the simplest, noblest, and most popular of all gymnastic exercises, becomes in Japan a feature of the circus, a fantastic and phenomenal struggle, executed only by professional athletes.

"It is true, however, that wrestling, under this unusual form, was among the most ancient diversions of the Japanese. But we must add, in explanation, that the national passion for gambling constitutes an important part of their interest in the performance. As they do not possess the institution of horse-racing — at least, in the European form — they have accustomed themselves to bet on the results of wrestling-matches between rival companies of athletes.

"The tribe, or guild, of wrestlers, professes to date its charter from the seventh month of the third year of the reign of Zinmou, the first Mikado, B. C. 658. As it is placed under the imperial protection, the corporation arranges its annual exhibitions with the co-operation of the government, sending detachments to all the principal cities of Japan. They do not possess a permanent circus anywhere: the booths or show tents are constructed by the cities which invite them, or, sometimes, the Buddhist monasteries. They are often of very large dimensions, but of the plainest character.

"The arrangement of these wrestling cirques is always the same. They rarely have more than one tier of galleries, which communicate with the parquet by means of bamboo ladders. Men and women sit indiscriminately together. With the exception of a small number of boxes reserved for the civil authorities, there are only two classes, the occupants of the galleries paying the higher fee. The spectators crowd into the circus long before the hour of representation. The chances of the match being the object of eager betting, those spectators who attend for the purpose of gambling in this manner, hasten to get possession of the best places for watching the performance, usually the lowest seat of the amphitheatre, including the arena where the wrestling takes place. None of the athletes appear in the circus until after the spectators are all in their places. They wait in the dressing-room, where they leave the garments, gird their loins with a silk scarf with long fringes, and adorn themselves with a sort of apron of velvet, embroidered with their coat-of-arms, and the tokens of their former victories. Different societies of wrestlers take part in each performance. The champion of each society is its chief, or leader; and he possesses, like the champions of English pugilism, a belt, which is usually presented to him by the lord of his native province. He wears this belt at the beginning and the end of each performance.

"The preparations for the match are interminably prolonged. Notwithstanding the assistance of their comrades, the famous wrestlers never find that their belts are drawn tight enough, that their head-dress is firmly enough fitted upon the nape of the neck, or that their aprons are properly displayed. Then they must carefully examine the articulations of their arms and legs, make the joints crack one after the other, and stretch all their limbs by means of pads of straw suspended from the ceiling. Finally, the sound of a drum is heard from the top of the tower, or rather, the high wooden cage which is built over the main entrance of the circus. The impatience of the crowd is lost in the noise of the reception, for all expect a scene of the most surprising character. The illustrated placards have excited the imagination of the public to the highest pitch. It is not ordinary mortals whom the spectators will now behold, but giants, colossi, fabulous heroes, who surpass all human proportions!

"Meanwhile an obsequious personage, diminutive in stature, but dressed in the most exquisite taste, and saluting all around him with the most perfect politeness, — the manager, in short, — takes his stand in the centre of the arena, where he announces, in a clear and musical voice, the programme of the performances, the names and famous titles of the two rival companies who are about to enter the lists, as well as the character of the bets which have already been made on the approaching struggle. The drum sounds a second time, and this is the signal of the grand *entrée*. The wrestlers advance in single file, marching with pendent arms, and heads erected, their figures towering over the spectators squatted on the benches of the pit. A low murmur of admiration follows their triumphal march. In fact it would be difficult, in any other part of the world, to arrange a procession comparable to that of the athletes of Yedo. From father to son, they follow an exact hygienic system, perfected from age to age, and the final result equals that which, in England, has only been achieved in the breeding of cattle.

"After this parade, the wrestlers divide themselves into two bodies, remove their aprons, and squat upon the ground, on opposite sides of the arena, which is a circular space, raised a foot or two above the floor of the amphitheatre. It is sanded, surrounded by a double embankment of straw sacks, and covered by an elegant roof resting on four wooden pillars. All the rest of the circus is open to the sky. From the top of the gallery the spectator may distinguish the roofs of the great city, the parks surrounding the Tycoon's castle, and the distant snowy cone of Fusi-yama.

"To one of the four pillars is suspended a sprinkling-brush: to another a paper bag containing salt; to a third a sabre of honor; while at the foot of the fourth, on the outer side of the arena, there is a bucket of water.

"There are four judges of the combat, each of whom posts himself beside a pillar: the manager remains in the arena. Provided with a fan instead of a baton of command, he invites a representative of each of the rival companies to enter the ring, and announces to the applause of the spectators, the titles of the two illustrious champions. Nevertheless, the struggle is not yet to commence. The art of creating embarrassments is one of the principal talents of the Japanese athlete. The pair of heroes begin by having themselves measured; which is merely a preliminary comparison. Then each one retires to his side, stretches himself, stamps upon the earth, drinks a mouthful of water, takes a pinch of salt, and finally prostrates himself in order to avert an evil fate. After all this they meet, as if by accident, and place themselves in position,—that is, they squat down, face to face with each other, and stare fixedly in each other's eyes. When they have had enough of this, they straighten themselves up with a great deal of gravity, refresh themselves again with water or salt, satisfy themselves that they are girded sufficiently, and begin to slap their thighs or knees in measure, lifting the right and left foot alternately at the same time.

"Finally they resume their first position, and, this time, pass to the second, always with the same gaze, the same apparent rigidity; but we notice that the body is raised gradually, the arms slowly extend themselves, and the crooked fingers are straightened to encounter the adversary. All at once the attack commences on both sides. Each repels the other's hands, without allowing his own to be seized, or without overcoming the resistance. The jury thereupon certifies that the two wrestlers are of equal strength and they rest awhile.

"Such was the result, and such is the faithful description of the first wrestling-match which I witnessed. Nevertheless, it was not therefore without interest. The trial consists, in fact, in pushing or hurling the adversary outside of the circle of straw-sacks. If he passes this boundary by a single step, he has lost: his fortunate rival is regarded as the master of the arena. Oftentimes one is vanquished so rapidly that the spectators do not perceive it.

"The Japanese wrestlers endeavor to win the match, less by their muscular strength and their agility than by their weight, — that is, by the violent shock or the constant pressure of one great mass of flesh against another. I have never seen one of them thrown to the ground. Lively, animated struggles, dramatic incidents or picturesque situations are very rarely to be seen. It also seldom happens that one of the two equally enormous combatants loses his footing, or is lifted from the earth by his antagonist. Besides, if there is the least indication of danger to either, or that the struggle is assuming a serious, passionate character, the little manager, with a thousand pathetic grimaces, hastens to interfere. The most he allows is that an athlete specially favored by fortune may seize his rival by the leg, and force him to hop backwards. It needs nothing more than this to excite the spectators to an enthusiasm impossible to describe. The conqueror is always handsomely remunerated by the society which owes to him the winning of its wages. The members throw pawns to him such as girdles or handkerchiefs, which he afterwards carries to the residences of the owners, who reclaim them for a stipulated sum.

"The wrestlers who acquire a certain celebrity are received in the houses of the better class of citizens, and even of the nobility. The government allows them to wear a sabre, on condition of paying a tax for the privilege. Children call them by their names in the streets, and when they deign to appear in any place consecrated to the popular recreation, they are sure to receive, from both sexes, a reception as enthusiastic as is accorded to any famous bull-fighter in Spain."

CHAPTER XXIV.

SCENES AROUND YEDO.

NOTHING would better serve to give a correct idea of the immense circumference of Yedo, than to follow the outer zone of the suburbs on the southern, western, and northern sides of the castle; for it extends from the village of Sinagawa, opposite the harbor forts, to the country traversed by the great northern highway, and the fertile plains to the eastward watered by two of the rivers which intersect the city. All this zone, however, presents the uniform appearance of rural districts attached to the capital. From one end to the other, the curiosities which the stranger discovers are of the same character, — rustic temples built against the sepulchral hills, statues of granite, or commemorative tablets, erected over the tomb of some celebrated personage, or meant to perpetuate the remembrance of an event in the history of the ancient Tycoons; here, tea-houses, great orchards, establishments of horticulture; there, sacred trees, resting-places commanding beautiful views, and sometimes an isolated hill, cut into the shape of Fusiyama.

This outside zone, called the Inaka, is like a park or continuous garden, dotted with rural habitations, or, rather, like a garland of verdure and flowers, which unites and binds together the southern quarters of the city with those of the west, the regions of the artisans scattered around the extremities of the main streets, the villages planted along the boundaries of the rice-fields, and finally, the dwellings along the banks of the Sumidagawa river.

During the season of blossoming orchards, the citizen, the painter, and the student become rural and idyllic in their tastes, leave the labors and pleasures of the great capital, and hide themselves for a day — or for several days, if possible — among the groves and under the rustic roofs of the tea-houses here. The latter are innumerable, and are mostly charming retreats, whose chief ornaments are the natural beauties around them. They are hardly to be distinguished from the neighboring country habitations, for their great thatched roofs descend on all sides nearly to the ground. Domestic fowls of various kinds sun themselves on the mossy thatch, which rises in stages to the peak of the roof, where tufts of iris grow and blossom. In place of verandahs, arbors of grape-vines or other climbing plants shade the tea-drinkers, indolently lounging on their benches. A limpid stream of water flows near at hand, beside the path which descends to the plain through gardens, orchards, and fields of poppies or beans.

The citizen does not disdain to accost the peasant at his labor, and to exchange with him many wise observations on the methods of irrigation, the quality of the productions raised in this or that neighborhood, or the state of the city markets. Often the Japanese cockney becomes quite enthusiastic, declaring that there is no such life in the world as that of an inhabitant of the country. The latter sometimes shakes his head, or replies by some joke in his own fashion. One day M. Humbert saw a peasant, leaning on his spade, with both feet in a swamp, listen smilingly to the sentimental citizen, then silently stoop down, pull two leeches from his legs and offer them to the former.

There are associations of citizens in Yedo, who three times a year — in February, June, and October, — undertake a veritable rural pilgrimage to the villages several miles distant, in order to delight their eyes with the changes of the seasons and the varying aspects of nature.

In winter, when the snow falls, they make it a duty as well as a pleasure to go with their families and witness the strange transformations in the appearance of the great statues or temples; but, above all, they visit certain advantageously situated tea-houses of the suburbs, whence they enjoy views of the shores and the inland landscapes, in their wintry garb. In the summer there are particular hills where the katydids abound, and every affectionate father goes there with his children, provided with little osier cages, in which they carry home some of the shrill-voiced minstrels.

The poets who celebrate spring and summer, and the artists in search of new inspirations, love to abandon themselves, from morning until night, to study and idle reverie among the cherry and pear trees, or the clumps of bamboo, orange, pine, and cypress trees around certain temples, which have been the classic haunts of the old muses of Nipon. At night they meet together in some favorite hostel, where the pleasures of the table are seasoned with conversations on art and literature, with music and song, the examination of drawings, or the reading of poems produced during the day. Sometimes a skillful artist will throw off, during the conversation, a rapid portrait or caricature of some member of the company, which is sure to be received with great applause.

The Japanese caricatures are generally very good-natured. Many of them represent scenes of ordinary life ; a grave physician studying the tongue of his patient, or examining a diseased eye through enormous glasses ; quacks performing the operation of the moxa ; comical scenes of hunting and fishing ; examples of female jealousy, and all sorts of household quarrels. There are also complete series of all the inconveniences of life in the higher circles ; illustrations of prodigal and avaricious families ; all the different grimaces which the human face is capable of making, and finally, caricatures of the artists, who are represented as painting with six pencils at the same time — two in each hand, and one in each foot.

When the Russian frigate *Diana* was wrecked by an earthquake in the harbor of Simoda, some Japanese artist immediately produced a comical representation of the event. The guns, spars, and crew were drawn, flying in all directions ; the commander with his drawn sword, hung, head downwards, in the topmast rigging, and over him was written : " A new way of keeping the perpendicular ! "

The Japanese artists also make use of animals in many of their satirical works. They will represent the superior of a monastery with a wolf's head, a group of nuns as weasels, or even the Tycoon himself as a monkey. One sketch of a hare prostrating himself in fear at the feet of a wild boar, gives the former the costume of the inferior nobility, and the latter that of a high functionary of the court, his head proudly bearing the peculiar mitre-shaped cap of Miako.

The native love of what is fantastic shows itself even in their religious utensils. The gongs, urns for perfumes, candelabra, and altars are frequently shaped like hideous monsters, with wings and open jaws. Their fondness for the suburban tea-houses does not simply indicate a love for the beautiful. Many of these houses are so situated that they command views of the mountain of Fusi-yama, and the outline of that extraordinary peak, as it appears at sunrise and sunset, in a clear sky or with a background of storm, would satisfy the most exacting imagination. But other tea-houses add to the charms of landscape the mysterious attraction of foaming cascades, mineral springs, or basins of hot water, as in some of the watering-places of Switzerland. The people do not resort to such places specially for the benefit of the waters; but they delight in taking their families and spending several days in those elegant cottages of cedar-wood, built beside the streams and in the magnificent groves.

Other places of pleasure are connected with some popular superstition. There the visitors may pass from the temple or shrine to the tea-house, with the satisfaction which follows the performance of a pious duty. At the beginning of the eleventh month, thousands of pilgrims of both sexes, mostly small tradesmen or farmers from the suburbs and the surrounding country, crowd the taverns and monasteries of Yousima-Tendjia. They may be seen marching in long files on the narrow paths between the rice-fields, hastening to buy bamboo rakes in that lonely temple, which is almost lost among the marshes to the north of the city. These rakes, which are of such good omen for the approaching harvest, are nothing else than holy toys, which serve as talismans in the dwellings of the faithful. They are supplied to the multitudes in every style, and adapted to the means of all; some are of colossal size, bearing a banner of silk or wood, on which is painted the Junk of Plenty; others, of moderate dimensions, bear the monogram of the God of Wealth: while the smallest have only the head of the God of Rice, or some sort of mythological emblem, in paste-board or papier-maché.

The peculiarity of costume, at that season, adds to the comical effect of the procession. The men wear blue cotton pantaloons and a wadded coat with wide sleeves; most of them are bare-headed, but have their noses protected by a crape handkerchief, tied at the back of the neck, while some wear a crape cap or a wadded hood which covers the whole face except the eyes. The women wear the same hood, and thrust their hands into the opposite sleeves to keep them warm. The same temple sells amulets to set along the borders of the fields, consisting of square pieces of paper fastened to sticks, and the bare-headed peasants carry them home conveniently, thrust into their chignons, like so many ornaments for the head.

Further to the north, the culture of those trees which are useful in the arts is as important a branch of industry as that of rice or vegetables We find there large plantations of the *Rhus vernix* (from which the famous varnish is made) and of the *Broussonetia papyrifera*, which is used in the manufacture of paper. The former produces, for thirteen years, varnish of the value of from twelve to twenty dollars annually. Incisions are made in the bark in June and reopened in September, for a second crop of gum; but the latter produces an inferior quality of varnish. As the gum in its crude state possesses poisonous qualities, the peasants who collect it anoint their hands and faces with oil.

The gardens of Odji, on the northern side of the city, are also a very popular place of resort. They are situated at the entrance to a mountain gorge, whence a small river issues in cascades, and then goes winding away through a beautiful valley. The balconies and galleries of the tea-houses overhang the waters; the rooms, the seats, the matting and screens are kept in a condition of dazzling neatness, and the service is noted for its simplicity and elegance. There are interesting historical souvenirs connected with many places in the neighborhood. A hunting-castle of the Tycoons formerly occupied the summit of one of the hills, whence there is a very extended view of the country. A little further, in a narrow valley, there is a temple founded by the great Iyeyas, and now dedicated to him, and a marvelous fountain which leaps from a high wall of rock. The deity of the spot is represented by a stone idol, before which the guests of Odji repeat their prayers, when, heated by too much saki, they cool themselves by means of this natural *douche*. In the village below, a number of booths or open counters offer to the visitors and their children all sorts of curiosities, made in the place; for the pleasure of such an excursion would not be complete to the citizen families, unless they carried home some sort of toy or trinket as a souvenir.

The gardens of Odji are all the more popular because, since the earliest times, they have been under the protection of Inari, the tutelar deity of the rice-fields, and also of the sacred animal which has been given to him as an attribute — Master *Kitsné*, the fox, who has deigned to honor this region with his particular favor.

He is worshipped on the hill called Odji-Inari. On the seventeenth day of the first month, an innumerable and motley crowd of people from the city and country flocks to his temple, to suspend their votive offerings there, and deposit in the grated box their tribute for the new year. Then, dispersing themselves among the thickets on the hill, they contemplate, at a distance, the great tree in the marsh below, around which, the night before, the annual meeting of the foxes is supposed to have taken place. They eagerly question the persons who pretend to have seen the congregation, each fox attended by one of those will-o'-the-wisps which the spirits of the rice-fields furnish as lanterns for the occasion. According to the reports of the witnesses concerning the character of the festival, the number of foxes present, the gayety or gravity of their proceedings, the peasants draw their conjectures for the coming year, and estimate the abundance and the quality of their prospective harvests. As a proper conclusion, they seat themselves around the brasiers in the guest-rooms of the tea-houses, and discuss, in a low voice, the mysterious influence of Master Kitsné in the affairs of the world.

"I have had the misfortune to lose a child," says one of the company. "The physician could not even tell in what part of the body its disease was situated. But while the poor mother was grieving, the lamp beside the corpse threw her shadow on the opposite wall. Everybody in the chamber noticed that the shadow which fell upon the screen was the exact resemblance of a fox."

"And then, the travellers!" says another, "when they see a road prolonged interminably before them, the distance of which, nevertheless, they know very well, is it not because they have forgotten to reckon with the fox's brush? How many times, too, they wander around between the rice-fields, following the treacherous will-o'-the-wisps, which Master Kitsné has sent to mislead them!"

"And the hunters!" exclaims a third, "what tricks has he not played upon them? If it sometimes happens that a skillful marksman dares to take revenge, he has only the mortification of seeing the fox scamper away, having caught in his mouth the arrow which was meant to transfix him."

The annals of Japan declare that Kitsné has the power of changing himself into many forms. When the Mikado who reigned in 1150 found himself under the painful necessity of dismissing his favorite lady, in order to save the treasury of the empire from bankruptcy, she vanished from his palace in the form of a white fox, with six tails, shaped like fans. The people also tell extraordinary stories of the abduction of young girls, some of whom never reappear, while others prohibit their parents from questioning them by uttering the single word: Kitsné!

When the fox chooses to assume the form of an old priest, he is then most dangerous. There is only one method of detecting him. Master Kitsné, whatever may be his disguise, never loses his power of scent, and its effect upon him remains the same. If any one places a rat, freshly roasted, in the way of the false priest, the latter, regardless of the consequences, will drop his metamorphosis in order to pounce upon it.

The priests and eremites of the mountains, therefore, know how to take the fox by his weak side, and they generally succeed in keeping him at a distance. But they must be continually on their guard to avoid being surprised by him. If the fox happens to discover their barrel of saki, woe unto those who drink the mixture which he leaves for them! Some of the most respectable holy men have thus become the laughing-stock of the people; a few cups have completely turned their heads. Throwing off their garments, uttering loud yells, gesticulating like madmen, they at once begin to dance in the wildest manner. Two neighboring foxes then appear and join in the dance, one of them keeping time by blowing into the sacred conch-shell, while the other flourishes the sacred sprinkler of the poor possessed priests. The countrymen also believe that when they happen to fall asleep on the banks of the rice-fields, they often fall into the snares of Kitsné, who deprives them of the use of their limbs or afflicts them bodily in other ways.

The Japanese literature, of course, abounds with fabulous stories of foxes. The hero, Kitsné, is not only a sacred personage; he is sometimes wholly grotesque, and sometimes diabolical. The common people have more than one game of fox, one of which is somewhat like our old puzzle of fox, goose, and corn.

The family picnics of the people, during the summer, are very agreeable. Generally two or three families unite, to pass an evening in the country, either on one of the shady hills overlooking the bay, or among the orchards of the northern suburbs, whence they have a full view of Fusi-yama. The porters go in advance to the place designated, and there inclose an appropriate space by means of screens of cotton cloth, stretched on poles. The ground, in the interior, is covered with matting, and near at hand are temporary fire-places, with utensils for boiling water and frying fish. When the company arrives, the ladies at once superintend the unpacking of the provisions and the feast commences. Songs, games, and instrumental music enliven the occasion; sometimes professional singers are hired, or even a pair of wandering dancers, who are also able to relate stories in pantomime. One of their most graceful performances is called the fan-dance, — a kind of pantomime, which is interpreted by a young girl dressed as a page.

There are also national dances, in which the members of families sometimes indulge. Ordinarily, the ladies dance alone, in a kind of quadrille, performing a variety of graceful movements without leaving their places. The men never dance, unless in a circle of intimate friends, for the purpose of displaying some extraordinary grace or agility, or when they join in the rounds, introduced at the close of banquets. In the latter case, the father takes his youngest son on his shoulders, and two other children by the hands; the adults follow, each independent of the others; the aged keep time, leaning on their sticks, while the nimblest leap and whirl according to their fancy, all circling around the table from which they have arisen. Some of the catches and refrains which they sing at such times are very ancient. There is one written by a poet who died in the year 731, and who thus celebrates the sweet wine of Osacca: —

"Tell me who was the sage who declared that wine is a holy thing. How truly he spake! Is there aught more precious in the world? If I were not a man, I would fain be a barrel."

One of the most interesting cemeteries in the environs of Yedo is specially consecrated to men who have distinguished themselves in the arts and sciences. One also frequently sees, in the open country, or at the entrance to villages, monuments which commemorate some historic event, besides the chapels dedicated to heroes of the time of Iyeyas. Buddhism has impressed its stamp upon every spot which can in any manner attract the attention of the people.

"It has been said," M. Humbert writes, "that the religion of the Japanese bonzes has been a benefit to the people; that it has protected its followers from oppression and mitigated the sufferings of civil wars. Certainly it has favored the agricultural development of the country, taken the trees and forests under its protection, and increased the natural beauties of Nipon. But, whatever may be said in its praise, the day wil' come when it can only have a retrospective value. When the age of feudal barbarism is over, the monastic system can have no further reason for existing, and the earth will belong to Labor.

"In the present condition of the monasteries, the impression which they make is a singular mixture of admiration and melancholy. When I recall those splendid pictures of sunset illuminating the orchards in blossom, the clumps of bamboos, a distant port of the bay, or the eternal snow of the great mountain, I cannot help associating with them the monotonous sound of the drums in the monasteries, and the painful indigence of the poor villagers. The works of man under the beautiful sky of Nipon form a shocking contrast to the works of God.

"The political institutions of the Empire confine the cultivators of the soil to their miserable huts, allow neither the mechanic nor even the rich merchant to live outside of cities, and inclose the members of the privileged castle within the long walls of their fortresses. But the religious institutions in both town and country have erected on all sides the walls around their monasteries and sepulchral hills. The interminable buildings which make the capital gloomy, are the frozen signs of a superannuated organization, which is condemned to die. Our cannons have not breached its walls. They are crumbling from within, where the breath of the spirit of the age has already penetrated."

CHAPTER XXV.

NEW-YEAR'S DAY IN YEDO.

"ON the 6th of February, 1864," says M. Humbert, "the New-Year's Eve of the Japanese year, I came to Yedo for the second time. The yakounins who met our party, allowed us to arrange an immediate excursion through the city, for the purpose of seeing the preparations for the approaching festival. The people had cleaned their dwellings from top to bottom, and put their furniture in the best condition. The side-walks were heaped with matting, screens, and articles of lacquered ware, bronze, and porcelain, which the owners hastened to restore to their places. In the houses of the rich, this labor was intrusted to coolies, who performed it with many joyous and grotesque manifestations, stumbling over footstools, tumbling down stairs, or tossing in a blanket some careless or lazy comrade.

"Others persons planted on each side of their doors young pine or feathery bamboo trees, which they bound together at the top with garlands of rice straw, ornamented with mandarin oranges and strips of gilded paper. They also hung the walls, under the balconies and roofs, with long bands of straw, interlaced with fir-branches and ferns. The shops, portals of the temples, fountains, and booths of all kinds, were similarly ornamented.

"This is the day when the carpenters raise the frames of roofs, and mechanics of other kinds return work to those who have ordered it. The streets are crowded with people from the city and country. The peasants lead their horses heavily laden with twigs of bamboo and young fir trees, while their wives go shopping. Visitors from the provinces arrive in troops, men and women carrying their baggage on the back of the neck, wrapped in oil paper, or silk from oak leaves, together with the indispensable umbrella. Everywhere, on the highways, the non-residents compete with the keepers of stalls: those who sell children's toys deafen the neigborhood with the sound of their trumpets, whistles, and tambourines. The venders of masks and fans arrange them in fantastic groups. The seller of little red lanterns carries a multitude of them tied to flexible sticks, balancing them in the air several feet above his head.

"The most curious variety of characters is seen in the streets. Four dancing priests make their way along, under a broad canopy of crape. A grotesque figure, with a dragon's head, dancing and leaping with wonderful contortions, and accompanied by a band of music, is an agent of the journeyman masons, collecting funds for their benevolent society. Among those who appear in the streets, clad in motley garments, with fantastic head-dresses, and masks with birds' beaks, we distinguish porters, cooks, and valets, in an appropriate disguise. They cover the head with a high conical hat of green paper, which almost conceals the face, and go from house to house singing, dancing, and collecting small coins for a festival fund. All the tea-houses are open to them, but under the pretense of showing them particular honor, the proprietors invite them into their own apartments, and thus avoid any unpleasant meetings of servants and masters.

"Nevertheless, the last days of the year are far from being entirely given up to festivities. The thirtieth day of the twelfth month is the painful time of settling bills. The master mechanic, the shop-keeper, the head of a household, in short every man with debts or credits scours the city, and works in his office, until all his accounts are carefully regulated, according to the rule, universally accepted in Japan, that no one shall commence the new year with debts. Not until this is accomplished, do they take their ease in the familiar restaurant, or join their wives and children in the festive preparations.

"Another rule is, that on New-Year's Day there must be flowers in every house. Most of the people buy, at the horticultural establishments, dwarf peaches raised in pots of coarse porcelain, and covered with double flowers. The Japanese have an astonishing success in dwarfing trees and plants, by allowing them the least possible quantity of soil, water, and light. Such is their liking for these liliputian productions, that in the stores for children's playthings there are microscopic imitations of dwarf trees, laden with flowers, made of cut paper, every little detail being exactly reproduced. The urns of wood in which they are planted are coated with glazed paper, which can hardly be distinguished from porcelain.

"The baker's oven also plays an important part in the innumerable preparations for the festival. It is a rigid rule in all families that their shelves should display an ample provision of bread and rice, for presents to the laborers and servants, and for the reciprocal gifts made by relatives and neighbors. In all the bakeries, the assistants, naked to the waist, are busy kneading, feeding the ovens, and withdrawing the loaves. The flour is kneaded in mortars with a pestle and the grains of rice are converted into flour in the same utensil. There are professional rice-pounders, who go through the streets from house to house, carrying an immense pestle on their shoulders, and rolling before them, like a barrel, a mortar to correspond.

"In the neighborhood of the Nipon bridge, the clamors of the crowd indicate the situation of the large establishments where rice beer is brewed, and the docks where it is shipped, by thousands of barrels, on vessels, to all parts of the country. Hundreds of coolies fill the streets, carrying barrels enveloped in matting, and suspended to bamboo poles. Those who buy small quantities of beer carry it in open vessels, and verily at great risk on New-Year's Eve; for the crowd increases, rushing from all quarters to the last auction of saki, and the best saki of the year! Thousands of buckets, kegs, and porcelain jars are piled at the corners of the streets, and trusted to the honesty of the public, while the purchasers hasten to the great court-yards of the breweries, where the saki is sold in lots, large and small. As fast as sold it is paid for, emptied into the purchaser's vessels, and carried home.

"The policemen, ranged at short intervals along the sidewalks, endeavor by their voices and gestures to keep the crowds in order. When their eloquence has been exhausted in vain, they plunge forward three or four steps and use their fans at random on the heads of the coolies and loafers who interrupt the circulation. Old men, girls, mothers, and children occupy the windows and balconies of the dwellings, and comfortably enjoy the sight of the tumult.

"They are not satisfied to retire until they have seen the procession of journeymen brewers. The latter, after receiving their wages in the morning, go out and celebrate their first day of liberty in the suburban gardens. There they have their banquets in the open air; they feast on lobsters, fresh cakes, and new saki; they pass around and empty the great bowl of ceremony. Then succeed all sorts of wagers and trials of strength and skill, until the fatigued foremen stretch themselves out under the cedar trees, with their legs luxuriously resting on the backs of the apprentices, while others move their heels in lively dances. In the evening, young and old return to the city, in a body. Their procession is a living parody of those of the daïmios, or princes. The herald-at-arms, wearing an osier chicken-coop as a helmet, brandishes in his right hand a dipper of saki, and pronounces in a hollow voice the word: "*Staniéro!*" (prostrate yourselves!) — the prince follows, looking like a Silenus, his arms supported by two followers. His convoy, as slightly clad as himself, also resemble the classic bacchanalians, except that instead of a thyrsus they carry a long wooden sabre in the girdle, and instead of a crown of vine-leaves wear a ridiculous mitre of paper.

"Such are the diversions with which the redoubtable brewers of Yedo terminate their year of labor. Their bacchic procession is also a public honor which they render to the sacred family of the inventors of saki. The god, the goddess, and their eight sons, collective patrons of the guild, are supposed to haunt the shores of the ocean. They wear a girdle of oak-leaves, and their long red hair hangs to their hips. Sometimes they are seen at sunset, on the yellow sands, flourishing bowls and dippers, and dancing around an enormous jar of saki.

"During the whole evening the sky and the waters of the bay reflected the ruddy illumination from millions of lanterns. The streets, squares, and market-places were crowded, and it was impossible for a stranger to comprehend the ceremonies which were being performed in all quarters. In the southern suburbs the Tokaïdo was very animated and bright; but gloom and silence began to fall on the neighboring streets. Here and there a solitary lamp showed where the teacher of the district prepared the poems which he was expected to send, the next morning, to the parents of his scholars. In order to accomplish his task with the better chance of success, he places before his desk a vase of flowers, and a dish filled with rice cakes,— an humble offering to the sun. He first writes his verses on a piece of red paper; but at the dawn of day, they will be copied on the fans which he presents to his patrons.

"When the hour of midnight approaches, we distinguish all at once the glow of small fires, kindled on the floors of the dwellings. They burn with a bright light for a few minutes, and then are extinguished. This is an exact repetition of the superstitious charm which is often tried with melted lead, in Europe, on Christmas Eve. The Japanese, during the last hour of the year, set fire to a bunch of twigs, sprinkled with holy water, and according to the direction, form, or crackling of the flame, draw their horoscope of good or bad fortune for the coming year.

"This is also the time appointed for the ceremony of purification. The servants of the temples dedicated to the ancient worship kindle great bonfires within the sacred precincts, and the priests, in their sacerdotal garments, issue in procession from the temples. On reaching the top of the staircase, they encounter two frightful demons, armed with pitchforks, which threaten to drive them back. But, thanks to the sprinklers of holy water, the monsters beat a hasty retreat, while the faithful loudly applaud the miracle.

"In most of the households, the evil spirit is exorcised at the same hour. It is the exclusive duty of the head of the family. Clothed in his richest garments, with the sabre in his girdle (if he has the privilege of wearing one), he passes alone at midnight through the rooms, bearing in his left hand a box of roasted beans, on a lacquered tray. With his right hand he scatters the beans here and there, uttering in a loud voice a caballistic invocation, the refrain of which is: 'Avaunt, Demons! Fortune, enter!'

"Everything being thus prepared for the inauguration of the new year, the inhabitants of the capital allow themselves a little rest; but at sunrise every one is awake and stirring. Men, women, and children hasten to put on their festival garments, and the first congratulations are exchanged between the members of families. The wife places upon the matting of the saloon the gifts which she offers to her husband. As soon as he appears, she prostrates herself three times before him, then rising to her knees and bending her body forward, — not a graceful position, but required by Japanese custom, — she offers him the compliments of the season. He squats down, facing her, with his arms hanging over his knees until the ends of his fingers touch the floor, inclining his head as if to listen more intently, and testifying his satisfaction, from time to time, by singular guttural sounds, long sighs, or subdued whistling. When Madame has finished, Monsieur formally replies, and then their presents are solemnly exchanged. The children come next in turn, and after them the grandparents. Then, having breakfasted together, the rest of the forenoon is spent in making and returning visits.

"All Japanese belonging to the intelligent and cultivated classes of society are thoroughly instructed in regard to all which good-breeding requires of them. No one ever confounds the persons to whom he must present himself with those who only require that his card should be left at their doors. Each one also immediately distinguishes between the cards which he should leave personally, and those which he may send to their address by the hands of a servant. The cards, therefore, vary considerably in form and style of decoration, according to the rank of those who shall receive them. They are sent in elegant envelopes, the largest bound by a knot of ribbons, and the porters carry them through the streets on elegant lacquered plates.

"The public buildings and the palaces of the daïmios

are decorated, on New-Year's Day, with the same materials as the houses of the citizens, but with this difference, that the pines and bamboos, bound with garlands of rice straw, form a sort of triumphal arch in advance of the entrance to the edifice, while the roofs and walls are not ornamented. In the centre of the arch is suspended a small symbolic trophy, surrounded with wreaths of fern. This trophy usually consists of a cake of rice, an orange, and a lobster — a curious tribute to the best grain, the best fruit, and the best fish!

"Such uniform decorations, applied to the palace of the Tycoons, have a character of noble simplicity, which accords well with the style of architecture. But the quarters inhabited by the daïmios, taken in their whole extent, are less attractive than ever, on New-Year's Day. We hasten to leave these clusters of barracks, prisons, and fortresses, this conventional world, governed by etiquette and duplicity, this cradle of implacable hatreds and sinister conspiracies, and return to the people and the manifestations of their inexhaustible youth and cheerfulness.

"What a contrast between the castle and its surroundings, and the streets of the city! The latter are announced at a distance by a joyous clamor, to which there is added a confused mingling of sounds like those of an æolian harp. This mysterious music proceeds from a multitude of paper kites, which fill the air over the city. They are in grotesque human forms, or cranes, parrots, and dragons, heads of warriors, or beautiful dames of the heroic times. A fine slip of bamboo, stretched across the frame of the kite, gives the musical sound. Sometimes the threads are covered with a coating of ground glass, and those who fly the kites engage in an amusing combat, each endeavoring to saw off the adversary's string. Young people of marriageable age take part in this game, and the crowds in the streets always applaud enthusiastically whenever a maiden succeeds in bringing to earth a young man's kite.

"On every side, the children have taken possession of the middle of the streets, for their games. Hoops, stilts, and tops are passed in succession from the hands of the little boys to those of their elder brothers or their fathers. There is a great variety of tops; those capable of the most capricious and prolonged revolutions are of cylindrical form, having a ballast in the inside which assures their equilibrium. The game of battledoor is a great favorite with girls and young married women. The shuttlecocks enter as largely into the gifts of the season, as fans. They are made of white wood, decorated with the painter's pencil. The shop-keepers of Yedo offer to their customers, as a gift, the choice of either a fan, a pair of shuttlecocks, or a porcelain cup. Purchasers, on this day, patronize only the sellers of sweetmeats, pastry, or children's toys.

"There are, however, a number of peripatetic merchants, some of whom sing and dance in order to call attention to their wares. Others sell birds of papier-maché, balancing themselves on twigs of weeping willow, and artificial fish, attached to a reed. At the Festival of Banners, in May, a huge paper fish is elevated over the roof of every house wherein a boy has been born during the preceding twelve months.

" Finally, among the articles peculiar to New-Year's Day in Yedo, there are eggs colored like our Easter eggs, bows and quivers of arrows adorned with fir branches, and very beautiful dolls representing a citizen in festival costume, walking under his umbrella, with a fox-headed wife, or a peasant with his agricultural implements. A special form of industry is carried on by the servants of the monasteries, who, wearing grotesque masks, offer slips of holy paper to be pasted, as talismans, over the doors of dwellings. Their comical disguise, which is very popular among the children, assures them a good business.

" Nearly all the masks and travesties so fashionable on this day have no other purpose, in fact, but to amuse the children. The latter, themselves, wear mitres of ceremony resembling those of the great daïmios; they hang themselves with brilliant trappings and mount as horsemen on the backs of their obliging brothers, while an adult member of the family gallops before them as a Tartar, blowing his trumpet, with a pasteboard horn and false rider's legs, as in some of our farces.

" Shall I speak of the curiosities displayed in the public squares? — of the puppet theatres, the exhibitions of magic, the drilled monkeys, the industrial mice, the intelligent rabbits? The mouse-trainer puts half a dozen of the little animals into a trellised inclosure, where they pound rice with little pestles; he takes the best drilled and hides it in the folds of his kirimon, then, turning to a table surmounted by a little temple to which conducts a long staircase, he places a box before the altar and in the box a piece of money, inviting the spectators to bet heads or tails. When they have done so, the mouse comes forth, descends his master's arm to the table, mounts the steps to the temple, opens the box, takes in his teeth the piece of money and lays it in his master's hand.

"The magician sells kaleidoscopes and colored glasses. To attract the crowd, he exhibits, in his booth, a heavy stone, clinging fast to a paper fan, suspended from the ceiling; a bowl full of water, in which floats an upright dagger, poised on a lily leaf; or four eggs resting, one upon the other, and supporting a vase of flowers. He also exhibits marvelous automatic figures; and then, taking a javelin in both hands he impales at random one of the numbered pasteboard cards scattered at his feet, the number indicating that of a prophetic page, whereon the purchaser may read his destiny.

"In all the lively circles of spectators who surround these sports and exhibitions, the first and the best place is reserved for the children. We see in the markets and streets, as well as around the domestic hearth, the predominant desire of the laboring, manufacturing, and commercial classes to make the first day of the year a genuine festival of childhood, wherein fathers and mothers have the first right. It is thus, apart from its religious signification, very similar to our celebration of Christmas Eve, at least as the latter is kept in Protestant Germany and Switzerland."

JAPANESE FEATS AT BALANCING
(See page 207.)

CHAPTER XXVI.

THE JAPANESE AND THEIR MYTHOLOGY.

THE Japanese people offer more than one problem to the ethnologist as well as to the historian. Many points will undoubtedly yet be made clear, as our chances for more thorough research increase; but at present the foundation of the Empire, the origin of the race, are involved in equal obscurity.

The first and most natural supposition would be that the archipelago of Japan must have been peopled by a Tartar emigration. There is evidence of very ancient relations between Corea, Japan, the Kurile Islands, and even Kamtschatka; for that chain of islands which extends northward, and then eastward to the American peninsula of Alaska, across the Pacific Ocean, resembles the dismantled piers of a gigantic bridge, and suggests the idea of a migration which must have been possible, even with the most primitive forms of navigation. But in tracing back the historical traditions of the Japanese towards their origin, we meet with no nomadic and conquering hordes, but, on the contrary, with peaceable tribes of hunters and fishers, under the name of "Aïnos," a native expression which signifies "men," scattered along the shores and over the islands of the North Pacific.

These Aïnos have not the oblique eyes, the high

cheek-bones, or the scattering beards of the Mongol race: they are a short, thick-set people, with large, round heads, and are specially distinguished by the remarkable thickness of the hairy growth which covers their skins. They seem to have been contemporaries of the extinct cave-bears. The few men of science who have examined them in Yeso and on the Kurile Islands, are of the opinion that they form a branch of the great Aryan (or Caucasian) family — probably the only branch which has been separated and pushed aside in the movements of other races.

Even as the Celtic blood gradually disappears from certain counties of England where it was once predominant, the Aïnos are losing the ground which they originally occupied in the islands of Yeso, Saghalien, and the Kuriles. They have so diminished, that their numbers, at present, do not amount to more than twelve thousand. Nevertheless, their history is held in reverence by the Japanese people. To this day, at their most sumptuous banquets, the custom is to serve a course of the commonest shell-fish, which is said to have been the primitive food of the Aïnos, as a souvenir of the ancestry of the highest Japanese families.

The Aïnos are never spoken of otherwise than respectfully. The equivalent of the term "barbarian" in the mouths of the Greeks is found also in the Japanese language, but the word is *Yebis* and not *Aïnos*. This, however, brings us to another puzzling question; for if the Yebis, with whom the founders of the Empire waged war, were not the primitive Aïno population, who could they have been? And, on the other hand, if the Japanese are descended from an Aïno ancestry, how is it that a portion of their race, instead of sharing in their development, have remained in the same savage condition as two or three thousand years ago? The study of the language will probably enlighten us on these points, in the course of time.

The cosmogony and early mythological system of the Japanese are somewhat mixed with those of the Chinese, but the two elements can be readily separated. The Chinese philosophers, for example, imagine a primitive, eternal substance, which they call Taï-khit, and which contains the germs of everything that exists, divided into two classes, the Yang and the Yin. The Yang is the active, masculine principle, or primitive force: the Yin is the passive, feminine principle, or primitive matter, — and all things in the universe are the result of a combination of the two.

The Japanese theory, on the other hand, supposes a succession of immeasurable periods of time, during which the creation of the world was accomplished in the following order: —

During the chaotic period, a divine Trinity began the work of creation, and separated the earth from the heavens.

In the second period, a series of seven celestial dynasties symbolizes the formation of the different elements.

Then, all the elements having been prepared, the definite creation of the world was brought about by the action of the last pair of celestial deities, the spiritual combination of whose attributes produced Japan, while from the deities themselves descended five generations of earthly deities, the last of whom was Zinmou-tenwoo, the founder of the dynasty of the Mikados.

In the simpler form, which is familiar to the people, there are many curious details of the creation. What may be called the "Genesis" of the Japanese Bible commences as follows: —

"In the beginning there was neither heaven nor earth.

"The elements of all things formed a liquid and troubled mass, similar to the contents of an undeveloped egg, in which the white and the yellow are still mingled together.

"Out of the infinite space which this chaos filled, a god arose, called the divine Supreme Being, whose throne is in the centre of heaven.

"Then came the divine Creator, exalted above the creation; finally the divine Creator who is the sublime Spirit.

"Each one of these three primitive gods had his own existence, but they were not yet revealed beyond their spiritual natures.

"Then, by degrees the work of separation went on in chaos.

"The finest atoms, moving in different directions, formed the heavens.

"The grosser atoms, attaching themselves to each other, and adhering, produced the earth.

"The former, moving rapidly, constructed the vault of the firmament which arches above our heads: the latter, being slowly drawn together in a solid body, did not form the earth until at a much later period.

"When the earthly matter still floated as a fish that comes to the surface of the waters, or as the image of the moon that trembles on a limpid lake, there appeared between the heavens and the earth something similar to a piece of reed, endowed with movement and capable of transformation. It was changed into three gods, which are: the August One, reigning perpetually over the Empire; he who reigns by virtue of water; and he who reigns by virtue of fire.

"All three were of the male sex, because they owed their origin to the action of the Divine reason, alone.

"After the three first males, there came three pairs of gods and goddesses, reigning over the elements of wood, metal, and earth.

"This second dynasty contained as many goddesses as gods, because the terrestrial united equally with the celestial reason in producing them. The first of the seven gods commenced the creation of the earth, and all together personify the elements of the creation.

"The era of the celestial gods, commencing with the first and terminating with the last male and female pair, who were called Izanaghi and Izanami, continued for millions on millions of years."

But the world, and, most important of all, the Empire of Japan, was not yet created. The account given, therefore, is very circumstantial. One day, when the god and goddess were sitting together on the arch of the sky, they happened to talk of the possibility of there being an inferior world. "Let us see," said Izanaghi to his goddess, "whether there is not a world buried under those waters which we see below us." Thereupon he plunged down his diamond-pointed javelin and stirred about with it in all directions. As he withdrew it some drops of salt water fell from the diamond point, and, condensing in their fall, formed the island which is called Ono-koro-sima. The pair then descended upon this island, and determined to make it the beginning of a grand archipelago, to be created by the united labors of both.

They first separated, one turning to the right and the other to the left, and made the circuit of the island. When they met, the goddess, transported with joy, cried out: "How happy I am to see you again, my dear and amiable spouse!" But the god, annoyed because she had anticipated him, replied: "My position as your husband gives me the right to speak first; why do you usurp it? your haste is of bad omen, and in order to avoid its consequences, we must begin our circuit again."

The second time, he spoke first, crying out, as soon as he perceived the goddess: "How happy I am to see you again, my dear and amiable spouse!" From this time forth, nothing interrupted them in the work of creation, which was accomplished in the following order: Izanaghi raised from out the waters the island of Awadzi, then the mountainous Oho-yamato, rich in fruits and with fine harbors; then the others in succession, until the Empire of the eight great islands was completed. The smaller islands were then made, six in number; and the islets scattered here and there formed themselves afterwards, from the mixture of the sea-foam and the deposits of the rivers.

The country thus created being desert and uninhabitable, Izanaghi called into life eight millions of genii, who descended all at once on the archipelago and produced an abundance of vegetation. Beside these, he created the ten thousand things, out of which have come everything that can be found on the earth.

On her part, the goddess Izanami created the genii of mines, of water, of aquatic plants, of alluvial soil, and of fire. When the work was done, the pair made their habitation there, and became the progenitors of the five dynasties of terrestrial deities, from whom, after another immeasurable lapse of time, are descended the races of men. Their oldest daughter, the goddess of the sun, is still adored in Japan, even by the rationalistic sects.

The youngest son of the last terrestrial god of the fifth dynasty subjected all the adjacent islands to his sovereignty, at the age of forty-five, and united them in a single empire. He was the founder of the dynasty of the Mikados, and is likewise worshipped at this day under the name of " the glorified ruler of the heavens." The date of his accession to the imperial rule, as given by the Japanese historians, corresponds to the year 660 before the Christian era. This is the point where their human history commences, although, for many centuries later, it retains a fabulous character. The very circumstance that the Japanese cite their early mythology as an evidence that they are not related to the Chinese, or any other neighboring people, seems to indicate that portions of it may have been invented for that special purpose.

Nevertheless, it seems very probable that the civilization of the Japanese, in its essential characteristics, had an independent origin, and that its earliest seat was in the central part of the great island of Nipon, near where the cities of Miako and Osacca now stand. The worship of the *Kamis*, or ancestral demi-gods (which must not be confounded with the reverence paid in China to the ancestors of families) existed in Japan as long ago as tradition reaches, and it possesses some features which are found in the religious observances of no other race. There are chapels dedicated to the several kamis in all parts of the empire; but they are most numerous and celebrated in the southern islands.

These chapels are called *Mias*. They are always built in the most picturesque localities, and especially where there is a grove of high trees. Sometimes a splendid avenue of pines or cedars conducts to the sacred place, which is always approached through one or more detached portals, called *toris*, like the pylæ of the Egyptian temples. The chapel is usually set upon a hill, natural or artificial, buttressed with Cyclopean walls, and with a massive stone stairway leading to the top. At the foot of the stairs there is a small building containing a tank of water for ablutions.

The chapel itself is usually small, and very simple in its plan, much resembling the native dwelling-house. Three sides are closed, and one is open to sun and air. The wood-work is kept scrupulously clean, and the floor is covered with the finest matting. The altar, which stands alone in the centre, is ornamented with a plain disk of metal, but no statues or symbolical figures are to be seen, and very rarely emblems of any kind. Nevertheless, there are sometimes stationed, at the head of the staircase, outside of the chapel, sitting figures resembling dogs and unicorns, which are said to represent the elements of water and fire. The interior is generally hung with strips or ribbons of colored paper, the exact significance of which is not yet clearly understood.

The chapels are also ornamented, by their pious votaries, with colored lanterns, vases of perfume, and of flowers or evergreen branches, which are renewed as fast as they wither. At the foot of the altar there is a heavy chest with a metal grating, through which fall the pieces of money contributed: it is hardly necessary to say that the priest carries a key to the box!

These *mias* were originally commemorative chapels, erected in honor of Japanese heroes, like that of Tell, by the Lake of the Four Forest Cantons. The prince of the province which had given birth to the hero, or where his deeds had been performed, took upon himself the charge of keeping the chapel in repair; there was no priest to officiate at the altar of the *kami*, no privileged caste interposed between the adorer and the object of his worship. The act of adoration, in fact, performed before the mirror (representing that bequeathed by the goddess Izanami to her children), passed beyond the guardian spirit of the chapel, and reached the supreme god above him. The chapel, therefore, was open to all, the worship was voluntary, and offered as the individual might choose, no ceremonial being prescribed.

With the introduction of Buddhism, however, an important change took place. The new faith was sufficiently incorporated with the old to transfer the chapels to the special charge of priests, and to introduce, in place of the voluntary, formless worship of the people, a system of processions, litanies, offerings, and even of miracle-working images. Indeed, almost the only difference between this system and the worship of the saints in Catholic countries, lies in the circumstance that the priests who officiate only put on their surplices for the occasion, and become secular again when they leave the chapel.

CHAPTER XXVII.

THE LITERARY AGE OF JAPAN.

M. HUMBERT has compiled a very interesting chapter on the introduction of literature, as an adjunct of civilization, among the Japanese, and the characteristics of what the natives look back upon as its classic age.

The illustrious Emperor Shi-hoang-ti, who occupied the throne of China from 246 to 209 before the Christian era, after securing his own power, cast envious glances on the islands of Japan. It was not a new increase of territory which he sought; he had pushed the frontiers of the Celestial Empire to their extreme limits, and was about protecting them forever from invasion by building the great wall which testifies, at this day, to the character of his reign. There was no longer a class of feudal nobles: between the Imperial power and the people, between the Son of Heaven and the hundreds of millions of his subjects, there was nothing. Even the opposition of the literary class was broken, the books of the philosophers having been reduced to ashes.

Nevertheless, the ambition of Shi-hoang-ti was not satisfied. Satiated with glory and conquest, he was devoured with the thirst for immortal life. Having been told that on the summit of a mountain of Nipon, there was a plant, the root of which had the power of prolonging human life, he sent one of his favorite ministers, the prudent Sjofoo, to Japan, in order to procure a supply of it.

The imperial emissary visited all the shores of the Inner Sea, without finding the object of his search. He finally established himself, with his followers, on the island of Nipon, abandoning his master to the universal human destiny. Neither he nor his companions ever returned to their homes. Through them the Japanese received their first accounts of China. The Mikado, however, was curious to learn something more than the information which reached him in this way. He thereupon sent an ambassador to the ruler of the Celestial Empire, to beg of him a copy of the annals of his court. His request was not only granted, but the Emperor sent some literary men with the volumes, to translate and interpret them. The Chinese language was soon taught in Miako, the relations between the two sovereigns became more intimate, and it was soon fashionable at the court of the Mikado to make use of the Chinese characters for the noble and lapidary styles, as well as to quote passages from the classics and to compose lyric poems in the manner of those of the Flowery Kingdom.

China thus exercised upon Japan a literary influence which may be roughly compared with that of the Hellenic culture upon Europe. When the heroic Japanese Empress Zingou conquered Corea, she brought away a great collection of Chinese literary works, books of the Buddhist writers, treatises on medicine, and new instruments of music. These were considered the most precious trophies of the expedition.

Their admiration for the arts and letters of China, however, never led the Japanese to esteem the Chinese people very highly. They continued to import teachers of the language, of music, morals, and philosophy; but the latter occupied a position among them, somewhat like that of the Greek Sophists among the old Romans. The studious, pacific, and mercantile character of the men of Nanking was rather a subject for contempt with the chivalrous and warlike Niponese.

Thus the Japanese literature, although developed under the influence of Chinese models, succeeded in preserving a certain originality. Nevertheless, as it was imprisoned at the court of Miako in the forms of a conventional society, it was obliged to move incessantly in the round of prescribed subjects, and to seek a perfection of style in the strict observance of academic rules. The authors composed terse distiches, as laboriously produced as the dwarf trees; they attempted to describe the ocean in a couplet.

The native engravers have preserved for us the features of the writers who excelled in this species of performances. Their portraits are always accompanied with the subjects of their poetic masterpieces. He who sang of the sea is invariably represented as squatting on the sand; another is lost in the contemplation of a fleur-de-lis; a third has a branch of peach-blossoms; and there are poets of rice, of the butterfly, of the maple-tree, of the crane, the moon, and oysters! We even meet with a young gentleman who has been carried down to posterity by a solecism. His father, eager to avenge the honor of his family in regard to purity of style, is drawn as beating over the head with a cushion the penitent son, who kneels before him.

There are some localities which are specially famous in the annals of Japanese poetry, such as Mount Kamo, where the great Sjoo-meï composed his book of odes beside a torrent, listening to the grasshoppers; and, near Yedo, the monastery of Kosseï, where the prince of Odawara found refuge on a stormy night, and, on leaving the next morning, gave the prior a poem inspired by his adventure, — which poem made the fortune of the monastery.

The literary intercourse with China continued for centuries. The growth of the Japanese in literary taste and in elegance of style was recognized by their neighbors, and in A. D. 815 the Chinese contemporary of Charlemagne and Haroun El-Raschid sent an ambassador to the Mikado, for no other purpose than to offer him a poem.

The cultivation of the poetic art, at that time, was carried to the pitch of heroism by a noble maiden of the court of Miako. The beautiful Onono-komatch is usually represented in her portraits, as kneeling before a wash-basin, and carefully washing from the page the lines she has just written. Her passion for the perfection of style was so strong that she never knew any other.

Although admired for her talent, she became the object of jealousy, and, being defenceless against the hostility of the court fops, whose advances she had repelled, she fell into disgrace, and was reduced to the lowest stage of misery. For many a long year she wandered from village to village, through the fields of Nipon, a solitary woman, walking barefoot, leaning on a pilgrim's staff, and carrying in her left hand a basket, wherein were rolls of manuscript and some scanty nourishment. Locks of white hair fell from under the broad straw hat which shaded her lean and wrinkled face. When this poor woman had taken her seat in the threshold of some temple, the children of the town gathered around her, attracted by her sweet smile and the fire which still gleamed in her eyes. She then taught them to repeat verses which celebrated the beauties of the creation. Or sometimes a studious monk would respectfully approach her, and solicit the favor of one of her manuscript poems for his collection.

The Japanese people preserve to this day, with an almost religious veneration, the memory of Onono-komatch, the wonderful woman, the inspired virgin, unassuming and severe towards herself in the lap of fortune, but gentle, patient, fervently devoted to her ideal, even in extreme age and the deepest adversity. She is the most popular figure in the poetic pantheon of the old empire of the Mikados.

The great literary age of Japan is said to have commenced with the reign of Tenziten-Woo, the thirty-ninth Mikado, who lived in the latter half of the seventh century. This prince took upon himself the task of purifying the national idiom, and the services which he rendered in this respect, as well by his writings as by his institutions of education, have placed him at the head of the hundred poets of the ancient dialect which is called the language of Yamato, from the name of the classic province of Nipon — corresponding to the Attica of Greece. The most important literary productions of his reign are, the " Book of Antiquities ; " " Descriptions of all the Provinces of Japan ; '

the "*Nipponki*, or Annals of the Empire;" a collection of national legends; the first great collection of lyric poetry; the "Book of the Usages of the Mikado," and a "Universal Encyclopædia," in imitation of the master-pieces of erudition and imagination in this line, already possessed by the Chinese.

In examining these immense collections, artlessly illustrated with wood engravings, many curious comparisons are suggested between the world as we know it, and the world as it would have been, had its creation and development been left to the hands of those Oriental philosophers. It is natural that the yellow race, with their oblique eyes, should be the Chinese model of human excellence; but their pictures of the many attempts which the Creator made, before he succeeded in producing this model, are truly amazing. They give sketches of men with one leg and one arm; or with heads having one eye; or human bodies on horses' legs; or with legs long enough to enable them to eat fruit from the tops of the highest trees, as they stand on the ground; or with arms long enough to fish with them in deep waters; or with a number of arms, heads, or legs, until, after many trials, the perfect Chinese human being appears on the earth!

The authors of this theory admit that no traces of the imperfect men resulting from the Creator's experiments are now to be found among them, but they point to monkeys, negroes, and European barbarians with white skins and red hair, to prove that they still exist in other parts of the world.

The University of Kioto, or Miako, was in all probability founded in imitation of similar institutions in

China. Nevertheless, the system of literary or scientific degrees, and competitive examinations, never took very deep root in Japan. It existed, it is true, in the eighth century, but that is almost all that is known about it. Japanese scholarship never exercised any influence in the administration of the government, or played any part in the national history.

Astronomy was the most important science taught in the University. There still exist very ancient astronomical tables, published by the University of Miako, and they are less dry and technical than most publications of the kind, for the authors have mingled all sorts of remarks and reflections with their mathematical calculations. They inform us, for instance, that in the year 202 there was an eclipse of the sun for several days in succession, beginning every day at noon and terminating at sunset; in the year 370, a snow-white stag was seen; in 640, a star was seen to pass over the face of the moon; in 646, the province of Etzisen was invaded by an army of mice, marching in regular squadrons, in an eastern direction, for several consecutive days; in 704, the court astronomers were favored with the sight of a *keï-oun*, an exceedingly rare kind of cloud, which denotes good fortune, and thereupon the Mikado proclaimed a general amnesty. The year 718, on the contrary, was a season of great anxiety, for a comet then came into collision with the moon.

The astronomers of Miako have adopted the Chinese calendar. They calculate a new almanac for every year, which the priests of Isyé have the privilege of printing and selling, by means of their agents, throughout the Empire. We find therein no chart of the winds, or predictions of good or bad weather, but a very complete statement of the combined influences of the stars and the elements, in relation to the months, days, and hours of the year.

With such a guide in his hand, each Japanese is able to cast his own horoscope, or conjecture the results of his enterprises. If he happens to be deceived, it is his own fault, for he has not carefully read or correctly understood the almanac. Therefore it is advisable that he should not read it without the aid of some priest, better versed than he in the mystic combinations. In fact, astrology appears to be the principal source of the priestly power in the empire.

However, in spite of the priesthood, the astrologers, the academic poets, and their conventional standards of excellence, the refined, artistic element which characterized the ancient civilization of Japan has been so wrought into the minds of the whole population, that its spirit is seen at this day in every branch of the native art and industry. All that comes from Miako bears the stamp of proportion, of elegant design, and the most exquisite workmanship. The classic age in literature was over long ago, but its influence on art has continued undiminished for more than a thousand years.

CHAPTER XXVIII.

POPULAR SUPERSTITIONS.

" WHEN the head of a household prepares his rooms for the ceremonial banquet which follows the New-Year's festivities, he is careful to reserve, between the last screen and the wall of the farthest room, a retreat, which he transforms with his own hands into a sanctuary.

" The altar is composed of a light scaffolding of cedar wood, generally two stories high, and covered with red tapestry. The upper terrace supports two idols of hard wood, flanked by two lamps of metal; and on the lower stage there are three small lacquered tables laden with the first-fruits of the year; to wit: two rice cakes, two lobsters or fishes wrapped in silver papers, and two cups of saki. On the wall behind the altar are suspended sacred pictures painted on linen, and on the floor in front of it there are two tall bronze candelabra, in which wax candles are burning.

" Between these candelabra the master of the house kneels, alone, or accompanied by his faithful spouse, to invoke the tutelar deities of the mansion. Nothing will induce them to forego this duty, even though they should be forced, at the most joyous period of the banquet to forsake their guests, and only see the wild jollity of the closing dances as so many shadows passing over the semi-transparent screen which conceals their devotions.

"I am convinced that the gods to whom the private worship of the Japanese is addressed at certain family festivals, especially those of marriage and the New Year, have nothing in common with the Lares and Penates of the Romans, who are called in Japan the *Kamis* of the house. The character of the former is difficult to comprehend; they are generally called gods of happiness. They seem to be personifications of human ideas of beatitude, such as the popular imagination delights to represent to itself. That is, at the side of their official worship and cloudy theology, the people have created a purely human and symbolical mythology for their own use, somewhat like that of the Greeks, except that it confines itself to types of earthly felicity, and makes no pretensions to an ideal of beauty.

"There are seven gods of happiness, and their business is to furnish to men the following beatitudes: longevity, wealth, daily food, contentment, talents, glory, and love. But it rarely happens that a family is placed under their collective patronage. Generally the common man is satisfied to invoke the god of daily food and the god of wealth. The commercial class adds to these the gods of contentment and longevity. These four, united, are called the gods of fortune and prosperity.

"The patron of longevity is naturally the most venerable of the seven. Having observed and meditated so much, his bald forehead is of enormous height, and his great white beard covers his breast. As he walks with slow steps, lost in his reveries, he drags his staff with one hand while with the fingers of the other he twists the long hair of his eyebrows. His principal symbols are the tortoise and the crane, and sometimes a stag white with age. His portrait is never wanting at marriage celebrations.

"The god of daily food is also the patron saint of fishermen. Yébis, the disgraced brother of the Sun, was reduced to the condition of a fisher and seller of fish; for this food might almost be called the bread of the Japanese. Thus he is always a popular divinity, always ready and cheerful. Daïkokon, the god of wealth, has not been treated very reverently by the native artists. They represent him as an ugly little fellow, with a flat cap on his head, and heavy boots on his feet, standing on two sacks of rice, tied with strings of pearls. His symbol — ironically, it seems — is the rat, the inveterate destroyer of rice and other property.

"Hoteï, the god of contentment, has nothing but a rag of sackcloth, a wallet, and a fan. When his wallet is empty, he laughs and gives it to the children as a plaything. He is somewhat of a vagabond, and the country people sometimes meet him mounted on a buffalo. They all know and like him; they show him the shady places on the hills, and the children go to look at him while he sleeps. If he awakes, he is always in a good-humor, gathers them around him, and tells them beautiful stories of the sun, moon, and stars.

"The god of talents is equally accessible to children, and he should be invoked in youth, therefore, rather than later in life. He is grave, and nothing can lessen his dignity. He wears the stole, cap, and slippers of a learned doctor, and carries a crozier to which is suspended a roll of parchment and a palm-leaf fan. A young doe accompanies him in his wanderings.

"The god of glory is clothed with a golden cuirass and helmet and holds in his right hand a lance ornamented with pennants; but he is rarely worshipped individually. He has no place at the humble domestic altar; but the Buddhist priests have adopted him, and they represent him as holding an elegant model of a temple on the palm of his left hand. There could be no more delicate hint offered to the rich nobility: the greatest glory, of course, is the building of temples, the endowing of monasteries!

"But the most remarkable of the seven divinities is the goddess of love, Benten, the personification of woman, of the family, of harmony, and also of the sea, that fruitful nurse of Japan. She wears the sacred stole, an azure mantle, and a diadem of her own hair, whereon shines the figure of a phœnix. I have seen her in a temple of that Japanese quarter of Yokohama which bears her name, with her head crowned with a royal crown, over which was an aureole of the colors of the rainbow, a key in her right hand and a pearl in her left.

"Benten was the inventress of the lute. Often, during the beautiful nights of summer, a celestial song, accompanied by melodious accords, is heard from the summit of the basaltic cliffs which overhang the waves; it is the nightly chant of the goddess, as she guides the star of evening to its place in the sky.

"In the eyes of the Japanese women, Benten is the highest type of maternity, the model of good mothers, for she has fifteen sons, all well-trained and distinguished, with a single exception. One is a public functionary, recognizable by his scarf of office; another is a public writer, carrying his desk and paper-box; another a metal-founder, and next to him a banker, with scales for weighing gold; then the cultivator of the soil, with his sheaves; the merchant, holding a bushel-measure; the baker, with an implement for measuring rice; the tailor, with a package of ready-made kirimons; the silk-raiser, with a basket of mulberry-leaves; the brewer, with a dipper and a keg of saki; the theologian, with the three emblems of the Buddhist Trinity; the physician; the breeder of domestic animals, always accompanied with a horse and a buffalo; the manager of transportation by land and sea, with a boat and a rustic cart on either side; and finally we reach the fifteenth, in whom the legend terminates with an enigma, for he alone has no profession or attribute whatever.

"But might he not have an implied vocation?— might he not have come too late, after the division of the goods of the earth, like the poet in Schiller's ballad? However strange the allusion may be considered, I cannot help making it; for one might well believe that the conclusion of the Japanese tradition is the same as that of the German poem, — 'The youngest, she said, who owns nothing, is he who possesses the most precious gift.'

"Such are the principal elements of the popular mythology, I might almost say, of the common, familiar philosophy of life, the moral influence of which, properly viewed, is probably better than any other in the world outside of Christianity. Its remarkable purity, its cheerfulness, its prosaic but sportive good sense, must have, more than any other cause, contributed to preserve the Japanese people from the decay with which it is continually menaced, under the immense pressure of Buddhism. Here, I am convinced, will be found the source of that joviality, that freshness of spirit, that child like simplicity of character, which distinguish the laboring classes of the empire. That which does them the most honor is the circumstance that the worship which they render to their favorite divinities has little of the character of mere superstition.

"The Japanese recognizes the children of his own imagination in the seven gods of happiness, and he has no scruples against amusing himself with them, whenever it seems good to him. He even makes them the subject of innumerable caricatures. In one of them, the god of longevity plays at backgammon with his friend Benten, and four of their fellow-gods, squatted around the board, seem to be betting on the goddess. A fifth, Yébis, brings an enormous fish, as a present for the winner. In other caricatures the seven divinities go through various adventures as travelling actors. The god of glory is obliged to carry a fish on his resplendent lance. Benten, in a tavern, displays her talent as a costumer, in arranging the wardrobe of the troupe. During the performances she sings and plays on the lute, and the god of wealth makes an accompaniment by striking a stick on his heavy wooden mallet. His symbolical rats act as jugglers. The god of longevity makes the necessary explanations to the public, and directs the performance by gestures with his fan. In still another picture, the god of talents is seen applying a moxa to the legs of the god of contentment.

"Many of the demigods and popular heroes of the old mythology must also submit to be grotesquely caricatured. But it is unnecessary to multiply examples of this kind. If there is anywhere in the world a people who have no more illusions to lose, even concerning their favorite idols, it is certainly that which inhabits the Islands of the Rising Sun. They are childish, if one judge them only from external appearances, but, at bottom, they are intellectual even in their public diversions, and still more so in their religious caricatures; for the latter are nothing else than a tacit protest against the ancient objects of their worship, and a tacit homage offered to the Unknown God."

CHAPTER XXIX.

THE NEW ORDER OF THINGS IN JAPAN.

THE remarkable changes which have recently taken place in the character of the Japanese Government, are due, exclusively, to the intercourse of the Empire with foreign nations. But the truth appears to be that there was an inherent lack of coherence, of unity, of true power, in the system established by Iyeyas, and almost any influence from without would have developed the hostile elements.

The government needed to accomplish two things: first, to assure the permanent and definite subjection of the feudal nobility to the civil and political power exercised by the Tycoon; second, to render the latter completely independent of the Mikado, in all temporal affairs. This second point, in fact, had always been claimed by the successors of Iyeyas, and the government was greatly annoyed when the representatives of foreign powers demanded that the treaties concluded with the Tycoon should be ratified by the Mikado.

The hostility of the native princes to foreign intercourse — since the more intelligent of them saw plainly what its final political consequences would be — not only led to the bombardment of Kagosima and Simonoseki, by the English and French, but was one of the causes of the revolt of the Southern princes against the anthority of Stotsbashi, towards the close of 1867. Although the Regent had made considerable military preparations, instead of opposing a vigorous resistance to the rebellion, he suddenly abdicated, and begged the Mikado "to call together all the grandees of the empire, and establish the government on a solid basis, to revise the Constitution, and thereby open to the nation that path of progress which conducts to power and prosperity."

The Mikado acceded to Stotsbashi's request; but the assembly of the princes was tumultuous, and terminated in a sort of *coup d'état* of the Southern confederates, who violently brought over to their camp the Emperor and his court, dispersed the friends of the Tycoon, and issued decrees abolishing the Tycoonate and conferring the executive functions wholly upon the Mikado.

Then Stotsbashi finally decided to accept the issue. The four palaces which Prince Satsuma possessed at Yedo, and which served as the headquarters of the conspirators of the capital, were attacked and battered down with cannon. The army of the Regent took up a position at Fousimi, to the northwest of Osaka, while the troops of Satsuma and the other princes in league with him occupied Miako. The first engagement took place on the 28th of January, 1868. For several days the struggle was resumed, with varying fortunes, until finally, in a pitched battle, part of Stotsbashi's troops went over to the enemy's side, under the pretense that it was sacrilegious to fight against the Mikado's banner. The castle of Osaka then fell without a blow, and Stotsbashi fled, by sea.

The confederates thereupon marched towards Yedo. Nevertheless, having been defeated by the troops of the Prince of Aidzen, they halted, and the more moderate of the opposing parties agreed upon a compromise. Stotsbashi was invited to resume his functions, but refused. A child, six years old, of the clan of Tokungawa, was then chosen, but the father refused to give his consent, and the Mikado finally decided to suppress the office of Tycoon, and himself resume the government of the empire.

He made his solemn entry into Yedo on the 25th of November, 1868, and has since continued to exercise the authority of a supreme ruler. Nevertheless, the pacification of the empire is not yet completed. The Northern princes, who made a bold stand in the island of Yeso, have been overcome, but the two parties, throughout the empire, remain of nearly equal strength, and the government cannot be considered as established on a permanent basis. The Mikado has been obliged to recognize Yedo as a capital (although he has changed the name to To-Kei), he has been brought face to face with the representatives of foreign powers, he has practically accepted the new relations of Japan with the world; and therefore, whatever change may yet take place, he and his court of gentlemen have learned that other interests than those of cock-fighting and foot-ball devolve upon them.

The most recent developments in Japanese history indicate that the prejudice of ages has at last been relinquished, and that, after a very natural but fruitless resistance, the government has succumbed to the new policy which events have forced upon it. Its youths are now sent, by hundreds, to receive an education in America and Europe; its half-explored mineral resources are to be examined and made available by the aid of modern science; and, finally, it has established a department for the improvement of the native agriculture, calling an officer of the United States Government to take charge of it. The apparent success of the Mikado has already led to the overthrow of the ancient superstition which encircled his authority, and his office is gradually transforming itself, despite the prejudices of the feudal nobles who support him, into that of a civil and political sovereign, hardly different from the Tycoon.

M. Humbert says: "The commercial relations of Europe with Japan are still far from having the importance of those which we have with China and the Indies. The commerce between India, China, and Japan and Europe and its colonies, counting both importations and exportations, amounted, in 1867, to about seven hundred million dollars, — more than double what it had been, ten years before. It is true, however, that the commerce of the principal Japanese port, Yokohama, has doubled in much less than ten years. It may be estimated at twenty million dollars, — comparatively small, yet much, when we consider the unfavorable circumstances attending our first relations with Japan. Indeed, when we remember the proportion of the population — the thirty-four millions of Japanese, and the six hundred millions of Hindoos and Chinese — we shall not only be satisfied but astonished at the progress already made."

"It will not be long," he adds, "before they will

seek our aid to develop their mines, to build telegraphic lines, and construct railroads through their territory. Then there will come a day, probably not distant, when glass will replace their oiled paper, when they will need window-shutters, curtains, and mirrors in their saloons; when they will light gas instead of smoky torches; when the fashions of Paris will have their imitators in Nipon, for some of the Japanese already affect the European costume, and the ladies will hardly remain long behind the gentlemen in this respect!

"The basis of the social order with the Japanese, as with the Chinese, is agriculture, which both races have carried to the highest pitch of perfection. In other respects, their capacities are widely different. One might say, broadly, that the Japanese have but a moderate talent for business, with a very great natural aptitude for arts and manufactures. The Chinese, on the other hand, satisfied with their traditional technical processes and utterly indifferent to progress, excel in banking, usury, and wholesale as well as retail trade. They are the commercial, the Japanese the artistic and industrial race."

We conclude with quoting M. Humbert's remarks on the approaching changes in the movements of the civilized world, resulting from the commercial relations which now connect Asia with America and Europe, and from the rapid growth of European colonies in various parts of the Eastern world: "It will not be long before a sort of Britannic Europe will be established in the southern part of the Pacific Ocean. This will act upon Spanish America as far as the Isthmus of Panama. All the region north of that point will be drawn into the orbit of the Queen of the Pacific, **San Francisco**, which hardly existed except in name before 1848, and now stretches her arms to Mexico and British Columbia, to China and Japan.

"This prodigious city must become the centre of the telegraphic system of the two worlds, communicating with Europe both eastward and westward. Since the completion of the Pacific Railroad, the European mails from China must necessarily take the route of San Francisco and New York. In a few more years, the centre of the commercial world will be changed: New York will have supplanted London. British genius is incited, on all sides, to more gigantic efforts. The Suez Canal, the progress of Russia in Central Asia, the turning of communication with China toward America, will oblige England to unite herself with India by rail, and to extend the lines, already built in the latter country, through Ava to China!

"Fortunate competition, noble rivalry of the Anglo-Saxon races, which, forcing them to multiply their attacks upon the colossal Chinese Empire, will finally — I venture to use a strong figure of speech — lift it from its ancient base, and move it to its proper place in the world of the future. That new world, which is now growing up, far from our old Europe, will be the grandest, the most fruitful of all the works of the age, and attended with the most far-reaching and incalculable results. The people of England, of America, and of Germany seem to have been chosen as the artisans of this great work.

"The Japanese have the noble ambition of emulating those nations which actually rule the seas and the commerce of the world. They may undoubtedly succeed in this aim, but only on condition of bringing an equal force to the performance of their task. Do they comprehend, therefore, that such a force can only be drawn from that fountain which, from day to day, nourishes the strength of Christian civilization? Certain signs seem to indicate an affirmative answer. The old Prince of Elsizen, who filled the office of tutor to the Tycoon after the murder of the Regent, wrote in 1864: 'Why should Japan refuse to follow the example of foreign nations, even in the matter of religion? If this should be judged expedient, it will only be recognizing our inferiority to those nations.'

"Such a change, nevertheless, would present unusual difficulties. If it were proposed, for instance, to translate the Gospels into the Japanese language, what characters shall we use? If the *hirakana*, it would produce almost the same effect as if, in France, the Bible were published in a vulgar dialect; if the *katakana*, it would not be understood by the masses of the people. Since the Japanese Government has opened schools of foreign languages in the principal ports, where the native scholars use the American manuals of study, it seems to me possible that the missionaries who have generally charge of these institutions, may soon attempt to introduce a reform in the system of writing the Japanese language.

"It is time to liberate the races of the far Orient from a state of things wherein the entire lives of scholars are consumed in learning forms and conventional signs. It is time to open for them a way to those easy and agreeable international relations, which now exist between the civilized races of the West. They **must,** finally, be provided with the means of creating for themselves systems of logic and psychology, a philosophy of history, a truly popular literature, accessible to all, and a religion which shall be worship in spirit and in truth.

"Our civilization has at last received the homage of the Mikado. The theocratic Emperor, who protested against the treaties entered into by the Tycoon, now takes upon himself the duty of causing them to be respected. The grandchild of the Sun who had decreed the general expulsion of foreigners, admits them into the new ports, the opening of which the Tycoon had delayed from year to year. The sovereign, formerly invisible to his own subjects, gives audience to the representatives of the Powers which have entered into relations with his Empire. The pontiff, who never went outside of his sacred city of Miako, now establishes himself for certain periods in the residence of the later Tycoons, in the midst of the *bourgeoisie* of Yedo.

"Surely, the ancient Japan of the gods, the demigods, and their successors, has ceased to exist and **will never** again come to life."

www.ingramcontent.com/pod-product-compliance
Lightning Source LLC
Chambersburg PA
CBHW020322240426
43673CB00039B/890